OPENING THE CORPORATE CLOSET

Transforming Biases to Gay Advancement in Corporate America

Opening the Corporate Closet

Kevin W. Jones
Dallas, TX, USA
Kevin@ConsiliumCoaching.com

Ordering Information:
Special discounts are available on quantity purchases by corporations, associations, educational institutions, and others. For details, contact Kevin W. Jones above.
Printed in the United States of America
First Edition
Softcover ISBN 979-8-8889-6442-2
eBook ISBN 979-8-8889-6441-5
LCCN 2023936067

Publisher
Dreamwave Press an imprint of Winsome Entertainment Group LLC
Sandy, UT

Acknowledgements

Thank you to my patient husband Simon for saying yes, every single time I asked you to read "just a couple of pages and let me know what you think." Your ability to recite every word of this book from memory will take you far in life.

Jared Rosen – you knew there was a book inside me, and you coaxed it out with unflinching support and inexhaustible humor.

The Economist and NPR would still be my only sources of news if Juliet Clark hadn't come along and made me broaden my horizons. Thank you for pushing my boundaries and buttons. And for making this book a reality.

If it weren't for the amazing editor Joyce Walker, you'd all be scrunching up your noses on every other page, wondering what the heck that last paragraph meant.

And to Pippa and Bertie, our crazy Boston Terriers: thanks for insisting I step away from the laptop to throw the ball.

Table of Contents

1

Limp Wrist or Stiff Upper Lip

What If They Find Out?

The junior high school I attended in the seventies was an ultra-groovy mid-century building. Its massive yellow and blue paneled exterior walls alternated with thin cream bricks in perfect primary-color symmetry. Floating steps expanded through massive circular slabs of suspended concrete patios flanked by breeze-block entrances. The interior was windowless, with fluorescent lights shooting in perfect geometric alignment down long locker-lined hallways. The swordlike leaves of imitation snake plants strained to reach the artificial light from the low rectangular brick planters that anchored each right angle of the perfectly square building. Mid-mod primary color mosaics adorned the walls along the hallways. A beautiful, perfectly symmetrical harmonization of art and architecture housing traumatic adolescent memories.

In between classes, those color-saturated mosaic halls were packed with pre-, post-, and mid-puberty kids. So crowded, in fact, that I never knew for sure, but I was always on the alert for whatever dangers might be lurking just around the corner. Usually it paid off. Like this day in seventh grade: I was walking down the hall to my next class. Girls passing notes. Boys punching each other's arms. Teachers on the lookout for anyone running. A few deep voices from the older boys, but mostly higher-pitched tones ricocheting off the tiles and terrazzo. Kids heading the other direction walked past me on my left. I knew or recognized most of them because we'd all been classmates, or a grade or two apart at most, since elementary school, each of us honing our survival instincts while figuring out our place in the food chain.

Coming toward me, there he was. Keith, failing in his desperate attempt to avoid drawing attention to himself. As I neared him, he caught my eye, this kid I'd known since third grade. This kid I used to play hide-and-seek with during recess. He almost never found me. Now he was only a foot away. He'd hit puberty early, God help him. He was a head taller than most of the other seventh graders. Taller than most of the eighth-grade boys too. And clumsy. Keith's poor limbs just couldn't figure out how to work together in version 2.0 of his growing body. Even without these physical enemies from within that called attention to him, the external ones always found him.

Drawing on my survival instincts, I looked away and focused on the lockers to my right, feigning fascination as I fooled myself into thinking he wouldn't see me. But he knew the drill. Anyone of us who was "at risk" would have done the same thing. What choice did we have? It was either him or one of us. Better for it to be him. So he kept walking, and I kept looking away.

Once safely past, I looked ahead again, not making eye contact with anyone. A few feet behind me, I heard the malicious cruelty from the eighth-grade boys begin.

"Keithy! There you ARE, you silly boy!"

"What are you doing after school today? Wanna come over to my place?"

"Hey, look! She dropped her books! Ha ha! Oh! She fell too! You ARE a clumsy, silly boy, aren't you?"

"Hey, faggot, we're talking to you! You're gay, aren't you? Where's your boyfriend? Maybe he'll pick up your books."

Their voices faded as I hurried away from imminent danger, knowing what I'd see if I dared to look back. Not that I was going to do that. Survival instincts and all.

Fascinating, this sense of survival. We're not fleeing saber-toothed tigers or angry alien tribes anymore, but that fear-fueled adrenaline still courses through our veins. So primal; visceral even. A surge of energy propels you away from danger, keeping you safe from the sharp tip of a spear or the taunts of eighth-grade boys. Even if running is merely picking up the walking pace, away from danger, down a fabulous mid-century modern hallway in a little junior high school in a medium-sized town near the Texas-Louisiana border in the seventies.

Keith was that one kid who the older boys picked on mercilessly. Why is there always one in every school, the weakest of the tribe, who provides easy pickings for the alphas? He was effeminate. He giggled, clutching his throat as he threw his head back in laughter. He did have a limp wrist, which fluttered about his lanky body as he gesticulated to the girls he sat with at lunch. God help him; he didn't know any other way. It was how he was made. Considered a design flaw in Southeast

3

Texas in the seventies and a huge magnet for these older boys with an equally primal instinct for sniffing out frailties in the younger males. He was first tier. Easy pickings.

I was second tier. *Somewhat* effeminate, I wanted to believe, but nowhere near as much as Keith. On top of that, my voice hadn't changed yet, so its high-pitched, pre-pubescent lilt was music to the bullies' ears. I desperately needed Keith around to take the heat off me. If Keith wasn't around (he seemed to be out sick a lot, no big surprise given what he endured), I or one of a half-dozen other boys would do. Even now, I remember each of their names and know where they are today. Aside from the mystery of what happened to Keith—more on that later—I was the only one who *actually* turned out gay. Back then, none of those details mattered. The bullies needed targets, and we worked almost as well as Keith. Those guys were at the center of the masculine solar system. "Normal" boys in seventh grade were somewhere in Mercury's orbit. We were further out, more in that of Venus. And then there was Keith. Pluto, at best, if not some other faraway planet since downgraded to a lesser status. The dreaded "faggot" or "homo" might come up in the derogatory more than literally intended sense when applied to us, or so I hoped. Either way, I suspect it was a finer distinction lost on the bullies, whose sole purpose was to single out the weak., They tripped us in the hallway, our books and spiral notebooks flying in all directions, when they couldn't find Keith. We ran around picking them up, laughing right along with them. Whatever, we were equal parts thankful for Keith and ashamed in our gratitude as we honed those survival instincts.

I paid close attention to the words, behaviors, mannerisms, and gestures those older boys singled out when they picked on Keith.

I stored the images in my frightened brain, filing them away for future identification and elimination. Praying hard to God to make my voice change ASAP, I helped the good Lord along with the rest of my transformation by taking those images home and practicing doing the exact opposite of what Keith did. I stood in front of the mirror, pretending to have a conversation while keeping a critical eye vigilantly focused on my hand gestures. Clutching my throat or covering my mouth when I laughed *felt* natural to me, but come hell or high water, it was not going to *be* natural. What was the rest of my body doing when I laughed? How about my voice—how was my pitch and pronunciation, within what I could control? Gesticulations—especially important. Was I looking at my nails like a girl or like a guy? Curved inward to your palm: guy. Straight up with palm outward: girl. Great—I'd been doing it wrong. More practice.

I wanted to sound like Johnny Whitaker in *Sigmund and the Sea Monsters*, a kids' show on Saturday morning TV. He was my aspirational all-American standard of vocal neutrality. I was never going to be masculine; I wasn't going for that stretch goal. I simply wanted to achieve not being *as* feminine as Keith. Not getting noticed. Passed in the hallway, invisible, with the rest of that mass of adolescent humanity scurrying to fourth period.

We were only in classes with kids from our own grade, which provided protection in fifty-minute increments, with the exceptions of choir, band, and orchestra. Choosing one of those electives dropped you right in with the eighth graders. I loved singing but hated Mixed Choir, which brought the two grades together. Another feature of our fabulous mid-century school was a set of built-in "floating" risers in the choir room. These steps did double duty as the practice area when we stood and the seating area when we took breaks. Sopranos on the upper left, altos to the lower left. Basses (relatively speaking—it was junior high, after all), upper right, tenors, lower right. Keith and the second tier, we were all tenors.

The core group of bullies was in there too. They were all basses—or wanted to be, which meant they all sang as low as possible during choir tryouts—so they stood guard behind us. When the choir director rehearsed with the sopranos and altos, we sat on the floating rows, providing the perfect setup for the bullies to start in on Keith. He was pretty much trapped, so their work was easy. They kept their voices low so the teacher couldn't make out what they were saying. They looked down at the riser steps as they spoke to him. No one looking at them would even suspect they were talking, their faces hidden by all that seventies hair. We, on the other hand, sitting directly in front of them, were close enough to hear every word. Variations on the same themes: he likes boys, he wants to see what they're packing, he hangs out with girls, he wants to *be* a girl, *is* he a girl, he wants to go out with them, does he like them better than girls.

Whenever I think of Keith and that choir room, the one thing that still baffles me is how the bullies never grew tired of playing this game. Did they even for a second wonder what it was doing to him? I know now of course that our brains at that age were far from fully formed. Cause and effect. Consequences of our actions. Accountability. Empathy. Compassion. All still growing their little neurons, connecting through synapses in a process that needed another decade or more to complete. Meanwhile, the bullies were completely unaware that they weren't even working on an open wound anymore with Keith. Even as they taunted him, it had already scabbed over, slowly turning into scar tissue despite their constant picking at it.

While they never grew bored, they occasionally switched their focus, albeit less enthusiastically, to us. I suspect we were all still works in progress in terms of what we practiced at home—the gestures, the voice, how we laughed. We weren't as much fun as Keith but we were far enough away from the sun in our fearful orbits that we'd do in a pinch. With us, the needling took a different angle. Rather than direct attacks on our sexuality (at twelve—geez!), the tone was more like, do we like Keith? Do we hang out with him? Does he try gay things with us? Do we want to do gay things with him? Were we gay together? "Gay together." I don't think any of us really knew what guys could do with each other, although we knew the only thing worse than being gay was being accused of being gay together with someone else. The term sliced terror through our twelve-year-old emotions.

We devised an array of denials, desperate to find that killer retort that clarified that we were a) not gay together and b) we were cool enough to joke about it. "You wish. Wouldn't you like to see that?"

"What's the matter, jealous?"

"Keith sits behind me in homeroom, but we're not friends, duh," we'd say as we rolled our eyes.

"Keith?" We'd snicker. "He hangs out with girls, not us." No, not good ole boy masculine us. We're just waiting for our voices to change and praying to God to let us act like the boys in Mercury's orbit. If God could please let that happen, then we'll be normal and never ask him for anything else ever again.

Keith sat on the same risers while these conversations bounced all around him. He heard our comments just as painfully as he heard the bullies,' maybe more so. He'd known us since elementary school. We had the same teachers, sat at the same lunchroom table, walked home together as we split off one by one to our respective houses. Those little boys, having fun and playing together, sweetly unaware of what awaited them a few precious short years in the future. The future that boiled down to this moment in the choir room, with the practicing sopranos and altos drowning out any remnant sound coming from the right side and the basses, with their bowed heads and newly gravelly voices, teasing us into shredding any remnants of friendship or loyalty to Keith.

He was entirely alone. There on those floating risers, sitting rigidly, eyes forward, never turning or acknowledging the verbal blows from the bullies or us. He never looked to us for help or tried to defend himself. We wouldn't have protected him anyway. We were too preoccupied with our simultaneous attempts at denial and impressing the older boys, who in turn only doubled down on their taunts if he reacted. So there we all sat. An isolated Keith, absorbing the deluge of abusive arrows that rained down on him day after day after day in this fabulous building. His former friends, seated on the risers next to him, growing further away and eager to disavow any past or present with him. All while the bullies having the time of their lives.

***

What is it about these primal instincts that drives us to commit what we think are essential acts of survival regardless of the cost? That helps rationalize all sorts of behaviors that we know instinctively are just plain wrong? And that sticks with us all these years later as guilt, shame for not being that one strong kid who stuck up for everyone else, like there always is in the movies? I never knew a single kid like that. I sure as hell wasn't one, and I didn't expect it from anyone either. Just as well, since no one stood up for me anyway. Our status quo was every child for himself.

What I couldn't articulate back then, in that 1979–80 academic year—the year before God finally delivered and brought about that much-prayed-for voice change—was that Keith was just a little too close for comfort for me. Any whiff of association with him would be my death knell, especially since I knew exactly what the bullies thought of people like me. And it wasn't only them. My family said it was wrong too. Our Southern Baptist preacher delighted in saying it was wrong, an abomination. And right at that exact moment in history, you couldn't avoid seeing Anita Bryant on television talking about how gays were grooming kids to turn gay—they're coming for your kids! I couldn't get away from it. It was a sin, and worse, gay people were, as we live and breathe, working feverishly to turn other people's kids gay. Monsters!

With all that coming at me from an infinite number of directions, you'd think I'd have successfully prayed the gay away. Yet, hard as I tried not to, I sat glued to our wood-paneled console TV each week for the opening credits of *Magnum, P.I.* I felt a funny sensation watching Tom Selleck, not Farrah Fawcett. I didn't know what I'd do with him, I only knew that whatever naughty thoughts I had were sinfully wrong. So I practiced my mannerisms and speech, "butching" it up (a highly relative term given the limited results of my practicing) to throw them off the scent. Despite my pleas to God to "make me like girls instead of Tom Selleck," Tom, with his thick mustache and dazzling smile, didn't bow out to make way for Farrah.

Since I couldn't do anything about the inside, I honed the outside image. Throughout the rest of my junior high and high school years, I developed a fierce sense of humor, made snide comments about the effeminate guys, joined the tennis team, and got elected to student council. I was POP.U.LAR!

Keith was still there, but making fun of him wasn't fun anymore. The bullies had found girls, cars, cigarettes, and pot and had lost interest in the juvenile sport of making sport of Keith. Occasionally, our eyes met in the hall, and it terrified me. He recognized me not just as someone he knew but as someone he knew who was *like him*. So primitive, this recognition of a fellow tribe member. He continued to fade into the background until, by the time our senior year rolled around, he was a ghost with a blank face and empty eyes haunting the edges of the hallways. His name was called at graduation, but he wasn't there.

I didn't stand up to those bullies; I didn't have the courage to confront them or deal with the taunting blasts that would almost certainly have shifted toward me. Keith took a bullet for us all. We repaid him by rejecting and denouncing him. Survival of the fittest. It was easier to join in on teasing Keith: if we were teasing Keith with the older guys, then we weren't the targets.

As the years passed, it got easier—not teasing Keith, but rather not being who I truly was at heart and instead being who I'd created. And because I'd created him, I could control him, control reactions to him. The funny, outgoing, popular guy who was in all those photos in the high school yearbooks. I was an officer in student council, on the tennis team, AND was voted most likely to succeed! Oh, and I led the opening prayer at every home football game. How *amazing* was I? This repeated process of voluntary suppression was fully hardwired by the time I made it to Baylor University (where, man, oh man, did I fit right in).

And speaking of college days, in retrospect, I know without a doubt that I chose a college that was certain to help me stick to the straight and narrow, literally and figuratively. My memories of those four years at Baylor are mainly positive: Wonderful times at dances. Laughing with my roommates in our cheap off-campus apartment. Socializing at the library when I should have been studying. Yet I can't deny the powerfully isolating feeling of loneliness that descended upon me when I thought too much about pretending to be straight for yet another day. Autopilot worked well most of the time, except when it didn't. I was a fun date and a great dancer (surprise!). Girls never worried about me trying anything with them, such a perfect gentleman was I. The implication of being straight while respecting womanly virtue was strong and praised, celebrated even, at Baylor. Who was I to correct anyone's perception? Being straight mattered. A lot. Especially with actual evidence of the pitfalls of being anything else.

In my junior year, the news raged all over campus: someone had walked in on two girls making out in one of the residence halls! Never mind that the dorm room door was shut, these girls believed they were engaging in a private activity between consenting adults, and this person walked in unannounced. The cat was out of the bag. Even worse, they were *sorority sisters*. It's cringeworthy to admit that I delighted in passing on this juicy bit of gossip. My fake shock and moral outrage were justified, right? If I was appalled by such sinful behavior, no one was ever going to suspect me of being one of them.

And besides, I was just one person—the news was going to spread fast with or without me. Such elegant moral relativism.

The consequences for their horrific behavior brought about swift punishment. The sorority excommunicated them, and while I don't recall the details of the reason, the school put them on probation as well. One of the girls ended up leaving school. The other brave girl remained and graduated, though the good Lord only knows how she managed through the next couple of years. Horrible all around, and I was right in the thick of it.

But that's why I went to Baylor, isn't it? This sort of immoral behavior was not to be tolerated. The university backed up its biblically held beliefs with swift and unapologetic action. I needed that discipline to help me remain the straight guy that I intended to be—straight, in a fraternity, going to marry a girl, have kids, go to church regularly, and raise those kids to be just as intolerant so they'd be ready to make fun of the next Keith.

This college scandal occurred over thirty years ago, back in the late eighties, and I think that context is important, so we avoid over-applying today's standards to the past, however unjust those actions. I don't know how the sorority or the university would handle it today. People, organizations, and institutions have enormously evolved their views on diversity, equity, and inclusion (DEI) topics since then. I suspect and hope that they would now address it with more understanding, tolerance, and compassion.

Regardless, at the time, it reinforced the horrifying moral state of my soul that being attracted to anyone other than the opposite sex was not only a sin and just plain wrong but also that being in such a decayed moral state carried real-world consequences. My authentic self took note and retreated to a space in the recesses of my brain that, when I finally blew off the dust years later, was barely recognizable.

The Risk of Authenticity

As a short-term strategy, "fake it till you make it" works well. Over the long term, when you don't allow yourself to think or feel authentically, anything goes. But then it keeps going. You add layers to that persona you started building out. It's a little tiring, then it's exhausting, but it's working! No one knows you're gay.

I'm not proud of how I treated Keith, nor am I ashamed. I was using my survival skills to make it through one more day of adolescence, and the only way I knew how was to sacrifice him to save myself. After more than forty years, I'm still in awe of how Keith managed to remain himself. I tried to find him online, but his last name is almost as common as Jones, so I came up empty. Just as well. I doubt he'd be happy to hear from anyone from his junior high days. I hope he's proud of each scar he earned in those terrible years. I hope any memories he has of sitting in that choir room have been supplanted by the joy of being his authentic self and that he never looks back.

I've met many "Keiths" over the years. And many "Kevins." Through various combinations of therapy, coaching, finding someone who loves us for who we really are, or caving under the weight of our false selves, we face the truth, finally, that it's not working anymore. It never did. It succeeded only in turning the damage inward so no one could see the hurt on our faces or the confusion in our eyes when former friends made fun of us to impress older kids. We might have deflected, but we didn't escape harm. The bullies weren't our enemies—we were, carving a false image deeper into our authentic selves that grew easier to portray until it didn't. Or until it was impossible to find our authentic selves under the cover of camouflaged heterosexuality.

Shadows of that self remain. As you'll see in subsequent chapters, it took a while and more than one coming out before I finally gave in to the exhaustion once and for all. Coming out, for me anyway, wasn't a matter of a one-off announcement followed by marching in Pride parades. When I told my mother (with the help of a gay therapist) that I was gay, she wasn't surprised. "Of course a gay therapist is going to make you think you're gay. It's like the fox guarding the henhouse," was the way she put it. On the other extreme were those who were excited to learn they had a gay friend. A bit of an accessory with all the colors of the rainbow. I was introduced as the "gay friend." Awfully cosmopolitan for a Baylor grad in early-nineties flyover city of Dallas.

Since then, Dallas has grown, been torn down, grown some more, expanded, built up, and evolved from that provincial town. So have the people in my life. I'm no longer an accessory but an old friend who still meets up for lunch every few months when a group of us can swing it. And my mom, well, I think there are times when she loves my husband a little more than she loves me. My husband, that amazing man who has put up with my Type A personality and quirks for over twenty years, even went with me to my thirty-year high school class reunion. In Beaumont, Texas!

That's not to say my guard doesn't still go up when I return to those familiar haunts back there, the birthplace of my false self. They remind me that across the expanse of more than three decades, I'm still not entirely immune from falling back into survival mode. When the waiter at the Cajun catfish restaurant there asks if my husband and I want separate checks, I wonder what's running through his mind when I say we'll have just the one. I drive by the evangelical church of my childhood, the anxiety building as we pass the old brick structure, even though I know for sure I'll never go in there again.

Back in Dallas, which is as politically blue as blue can be in a red state, I wonder why, upon noticing my wedding ring, I let that Uber driver ask how long my wife and I have been married without correcting him. Why I let the massage therapist rant about Adam and Eve, not Adam and Steve. Why I didn't speak up when the guy next to me on a pre-pandemic flight talked about these special rights that "the gays" have now that they can marry. Suffice it to say, I was not true to my authentic self, my husband, or my marriage. Hardwiring. Lying by omission. This, despite working at a place where I feel entirely comfortable being my authentic self. Real, perceived, or somewhere in between, I'm not immune from making split-second cost-benefit analyses of authenticity.

Here's the thing: I can make a watertight, logical argument that you should be able to feel 100 percent comfortable being your authentic self where you work and ignore the world beyond those virtual work walls that isn't so friendly—where people sneer when they talk about Adam and Steve, where people claim we've gone too far with these special rights. But that logic crashes head-on into a reality that is a heartbreaking contrast to mine for many people in the gay community. So the grown-up "Keiths" and "Kevins" today still make millions of microscopic decisions about themselves and others based on the threat level of the situations they find themselves in. We came out. We got therapy. We took shit from others while educating them. We waited for time to crawl forward so that the world around us might change. It's better for us than it was for the people at Stonewall. It's no longer illegal to be gay. We can get married. But rights that are given can be taken away, so the threat level remains.

One of my coaching clients is a prime example. Patrick's (not his real name) work environment was inclusive, diverse, and supportive. He felt like he belonged. His husband joined him for work-related events, and he talked about his personal life freely. He was a notable example of what can happen when an organization creates a safe environment that allows employees to bring their full selves to work. However, one of Patrick's external clients' companies wasn't as far along on the DEI continuum as his employer. In fact, it didn't sound like you could even locate them on it. The company president held optional Bible studies, which, of course, everyone attended. There were no policies, even at the most fundamental level, that mentioned what an inclusive environment might consist of in their workplace.

At a work-related dinner, after a couple of drinks, Patrick's contact's lips loosened. She was as open-minded as the next person, and she had no problem if someone wanted to embrace "that lifestyle," but her religion was clear on the definition of marriage, and it was between one man and one woman. A sacred sacrament that should not be mocked by two women walking down the aisle, especially when it was a **church** aisle. Her spiritual beliefs were clear on that point. Things had finally gone just too far. She didn't know Patrick was gay and would have likely been horrified if she knew she was making him uncomfortable. Yet she was comfortable enough in her opinions to share them freely without considering how it might affect him. In every other way, they had built a great working relationship, but now the guard was back up. Before that dinner, Patrick had listened to that quiet voice cautioning him against talking about his husband with her. She was a nice person. They had a few hobbies and interests in common. He felt like he knew her—until that dinner. Until then, he'd wanted to share more about his personal life with her, to trust her. But as quiet as it was, that voice was insistent, so he didn't. That evening, her comments reinforced to him that you can never be too careful about this sort of thing. To him, they proved the value and necessity of keeping that guard up.

Patrick was disappointed in himself when he shared this story because, in his words, he had taken a step backward. He went back into the closet when it came to this relationship because of his fear that telling her he was gay **and married** might jeopardize their working relationship. That could, in turn, affect her desire to continue having him as her point of contact, affecting his company's perception of his performance.

But if his work environment is as inclusive, diverse, and supportive as it appears, surely they'd stand up for him if he made his concerns known, right? Not so fast. They might. But organizations are no less immune to breaches of authenticity than humans. They can sincerely mean it when they talk about their inclusive and supportive culture and policies. The absolute sincerity in encouraging their people to bring their full selves to work, physically or virtually, is unquestionable *when they say it*. Yet, faced with the potential of one unhappy employee or an unhappy client, especially if that client happens to have deep pockets, the decision, though unpleasant, could just as easily favor the client as the employee. It's critically important that we listen to what organizations say. But what they *do* repeatedly after *saying* what they say matters more.

Speechless for 15 Seconds

Peering back into the early nineties, I'm amazed by my work ethic, or lack of one. I arrived somewhere around eight and left promptly at five. So did most of the people in my group of technical writers. In terms of our structure, we were way back-office. We didn't worry about often-missed deadlines because we blamed the developers or the marketing department. I'm sure there were some employees who weren't clock-watchers, but we didn't know them.

Besides watching the clock for leaving time to roll around, we watched it with equal fervor for noon, when we went to lunch together. We didn't socialize outside of the office, but considering we spent most of our workdays chatting with each other in addition to our hour-plus lunches, we had a lot of time to get to know each other.

From a demographic and experience perspective, we were a diverse group. At twenty-five, I was the youngster, while a woman who saw the retirement light at the end of the tunnel was at the other end of the age spectrum. There was everything in between: men, women, Black, white, old, young. And the assumption was that everyone was straight.

Even now, I'm stunned at the amount of money I spent eating out when I was in my twenties. I lived in a one-bedroom apartment and drove a used, paid-for Honda Accord, the model where the headlights flipped open like eyes when you turned them on. I didn't bother saving for retirement, which was a bazillion years in the future. So yeah, fair to say I had a decent amount of disposable income. I try not to think about how much money I spent on those lunches with coworkers and what that money would be worth now if I had invested it instead.

Anyway, our office was in a suburb of Dallas. Back then, options within a decent radius were Tex-Mex, Chinese buffets, and national chains with spiral-bound books for menus. In a post-COVID-19 world, the thought of buffets sort of grosses me out now—all those people breathing over open chafing dishes heated to a tepid temperature by cans of Sterno underneath. Back in those days, it didn't faze me or anyone else in the packed restaurant as we breathed, coughed, and sneezed our way through the super-Americanized variants of Chinese food (who knew the fortune cookie was *not* authentic?).

One day, I was returning to our table of seven or eight with my second plate of whatever from the buffet. I don't remember the conversation they were having when I'd left to get more food. But the one I returned to is as vivid now as the day I first heard it.

Our group manager, Jeff, was a nice enough guy in his early-to-mid thirties. His wife had left him a couple of years earlier. She had told him he was too boring. Though I had no knowledge of their home life, I can't imagine someone saying something that cruel to the person they vowed to love and cherish. Whatever he was at home, he was funny and entertaining at work. Maybe needing to be the center of attention a little too much, but not enough to be a dick about it. He shared stories about his time in the military, and he made us laugh at his dead-on imitations of people ranging from the famous to coworkers two cubicle rows away.

Heading back to the table, I noticed Jeff was holding court with an entertaining story, but I couldn't make out what he was saying above the din of a dozen conversations and clattering cutlery ricocheting off the concrete floor and bare walls. As I neared the table and the conversation level grew intelligible, I heard him talking about someone we knew at the company—the general data points: the group he was in, which floor, physical attributes, that sort of thing. No one was looking at me as I sat down at the other end of the table. All eyes were on Jeff as he continued: He'd heard things about this guy. Had anyone else? Pretty obvious from the way he dressed and spoke, right? He'd heard he was trying to start a group of them. Some sort of support group. Who the hell would support that, and why would anyone want to be part of something as disgusting as that anyway? But it figured it was this guy who wanted to start it, Jeff surmised. He was, you know, that way. At that point, he raised his arm, letting his wrist go limp and flop up and down a few times to emphasize the "you know."

He smiled. The gang laughed—some guffawed, a couple chuckled nervously as they looked my way when Jeff wasn't looking at them. My face was on fire as I slapped my knee and laughed along with them. *Why were they looking at me? I wasn't gay. Good lord, no, not me. No sir. Not one bit. That's not why they were looking at me. Probably it was because I had just sat back down. That's what they noticed. Had to be because no one knew—spoiler alert—that I really was gay.* Dun dun dunnnn!

Even as I was the last one to stop laughing, I was horrified and crushed. This man I knew—thought I knew—was talking about me. Not me, but me. The me back then, who could have avoided such ugly situations by bringing a sandwich to eat at his desk and investing that lunch money instead. I wish I could go back to that me and tell him what a jerk Jeff was. That it wasn't about me but about his own insecurities and need for attention. That I was fine the way I was. Instead, knowing what I now knew about how he thought about people like me, I felt inferior, like I didn't deserve to be part of this group because I wasn't like them in the way that I so desperately wanted to be. Still, why were Susan and Brian looking at me, really? I made a note-to-self to analyze sketchy actions and work on them.

***

Turned out this was not to be a one-off. Once Jeff found success in milking gay-themed laughs, he incorporated them into his act. He added a gay voice to his limp-wrist imitations of the guys who were "light in the loafers," as he put it. The speculation around who else might be gay was a standing theme. The "Men on Film" sketches from the popular Sunday night show *In Living Color* were quoted verbatim on Mondays. I wonder if he was dealing with his own sexuality issues. That, or he was an insensitive jerk. Either way, the laughs dwindled over the next few weeks as he tried harder. I wasn't the only one—we were all getting tired of the same old schtick.

The floor we worked on was a big open-plan space. We didn't have the long tables and flat-screen monitors like people in open-plan offices had to deal with just before the pandemic. Rather, it was an open floor plan in the sense that if you stood up in your cubicle, you could see from one end of the floor to the other with nothing to obstruct your view. You could pop your head up to see what was going on—I think that's where the term "prairie-dogging" originated, right?

The cubicles were higher back then, and their walls were lined with padding and heavy fabric, so at least the sound levels were low enough to allow you to do your work—unless someone was having a conversation in the cubicle right next to yours, which was happening on that eventful day. I was at my computer—big old white Apple integrated CPU and monitor with a 5 ¼ floppy disk drive—when I heard Jeff approach Brian's cubicle, which was next door to mine. The conversation began with work-related something or other, and I tuned them out. I don't remember how long I was working on some user manual or another when I picked up snippets of their chat, which had moved on from work.

As Jeff had so eloquently noted, around this time the company was indeed allowing people to form special interest groups. Minorities in technology, working mothers, Bible studies. Jeff, as he relayed to Brian, and which I overheard, couldn't believe his ears when he confirmed his earlier suspicions that a *gay* group *was* forming. "What was that even going to be, like, a group of six? And what were they going to talk about—new outfits and cute guys at work?" he wondered out loud, re-energized with all this new material.

I tried to focus on work, but it was impossible. Brian laughed politely a couple of times. Jeff continued. "They should have an exclusive group for straight men. Who wants to be associated with a group like that anyway?"

I felt my face flush again, no doubt turning bright red. This time I wasn't embarrassed, I was pissed! As the adrenaline kicked in, I rolled back from my desk and stood up prairie-dog style. I didn't make any other moves. I just stood in place, staring across the cube wall, only my head visible to Jeff and Brian. Making no attempt to interrupt their conversation, I listened silently until Brian noticed something—me—out of the corner of his eye.

He turned to me and asked whether they were being too loud and gave a preemptive apology. No, no, I told him. Their volume wasn't bothering me. I just had a quick question for Jeff.

"What difference does it make to you if a gay group exists here, Jeff?" I'm not paraphrasing. I remember those exact words. And I remember the slack-jawed look on Jeff's face. It was many looks that morphed one into the next. Confusion about the question, followed by surprise, intent to respond, pause, contemplation, analysis, and slow realization. Then the beautiful CYA mode kicked in. He didn't really care. People can do whatever they want. It's none of his business. He was just joking around. "And besides, why did *you* care?" I think that last bit just popped out, given he'd already figured it out.

"You get that I'm gay, right Jeff?" I asked, holding steady. At least the part of me that they could see above the cube wall. My hands shook. Sweat dripped off my forehead into my eyes. Brian, seizing a perfect opportunity to keep his mouth shut, studied the carpet pattern under his feet. I felt the weight of what I'd said and didn't care. I'd packed a wallop and knew it.

From there, I remember emotions and themes—no exact words. After maybe fifteen seconds without saying a word, Jeff cobbled together a few excuses: He didn't know. How could he? I'd never said anything. He didn't mean to offend me. Why am I being so sensitive about it now? It's not that big of a deal. He was only joking.

I didn't care what he was saying. The weight of that dark closet was floating off and away from me, and I felt like I was going to sail out the window next to my cubicle right along with it.

"Well, now you know. I'm gay. I don't want to hear this anymore." I sat down, rolled back up to my monitor, and listened to the beautiful silence on the other side as Brian turned back to his work and Jeff padded quietly away.

Even now, I can recount most of the details of how the rest of that day unfolded. Strange how the mind works when something big happens in your life. It freezes not only that moment, but it captures the side gigs too. No one said anything to me. Nothing dramatic happened. I wasn't called into an office.

With seven words, I had blasted the door off my self-imposed corporate closet. I was out.

Normalizing Your Suppressed Feelings

It's not like it was the first time I'd overheard people talking about gays in pretty much the same way Jeff had. Why was this situation the final straw? Pretty simple: I was exhausted. For eight hours a day, five days a week, fifty weeks a year (only two weeks' vacation back then)—or around 2,000 hours—I had been hiding a core part of myself. Not to mention the 25 years 24/7 up to that point. The persistent questioning myself: Does anyone suspect? Am I doing, saying, thinking anything that might arouse suspicion? Do they not suspect? What am I doing *right* that I should keep doing? The constant wondering: How am I speaking, walking, gesturing? The words I use, clothes I wear. Navigating dating (I could write a second book on that topic alone). What lines did I risk crossing and where are they? What were the details of that made-up story I told, and who all did I tell it to? The pleading: Uh-oh, there's that guy walking toward me on campus. Please, God, don't let him say anything in front of my friends. I'll never do it again. It was just that one time, and I was weak. Please, just make him keep walking past me. I'm not like him, I promise.

Back in seventh-grade English, Mrs. Rowe had given us an assignment: write about what your family will be like in twenty-five years. No, not your current family—your family once you were married.

This assignment was exciting because I already visualized my family and knew my future wife's name: Joanne. Joanne and I drove flying cars in 2004. We had three children and a dog. Our house looked just like the Brady Bunch's house. I was a surgeon. Joanne didn't have to work, but she really loved her volunteer work with the Junior League. She had a short Dorothy Hamill haircut accessorized with colorful scarves. I loved buying scarves for her, knowing how happy they made her. My parents loved her, as did my siblings, who were all happily married as well, with kids of their own. We often had other happily married straight couples over for cookouts. They all brought their kids, who were best friends with ours. They played in the pool while the adults sat around drinking martinis and smoking cigarettes. The men sat in comfy chairs while the women perched on the armrests of their husbands' chairs, leaning back and into their men.

Joanne was the most amazing hostess—it's why she was the social secretary of the Junior League. With the help of our maid, she was ever alert to empty glasses and full ashtrays. And what a fantastic conversationalist! At the end of these fun-filled heterosexual evenings, which always went late into the evening because people just hated to leave, I congratulated her on yet another successful party as we walked arm-in-arm to our master suite, complete with a jacuzzi tub, leaving the maid to clean up the mess.

My aspirational life with Joanne was key to building, maintaining, and evolving my straight persona out of junior high and on to high school, college, and beyond. She was the embodiment of everything perfect about my future life. Though the details about her faded over time, the imperative of spending my life with her strengthened with every decision I made about how I represented myself to others. Play a sport in high school—check (tennis, but that counts). Have a girlfriend—check (in the sense that I hung out with a few girls and allowed speculation that I might be dating one of them). Join a fraternity in college—check. Be seen making out with girls at fraternity dances—check (it might have been a Tri-Delt in my arms, but it was a young Alec Baldwin from *Knots Landing* in my mind).

On and on. It felt right. Wanting to do all these straight things and marrying my Joanne felt *normal*. I wasn't suppressing anything since I wasn't gay anyway. God will fix me once I was married. Like anything worth having, it was simply a matter of work, practice, and commitment. That's all. All I had to do was focus on that space-age future with Joanne, every hour of every day of every month of every year, and remain vigilant, guarded, aware, protected, suspicious, anticipatory. Stay two steps ahead of what friends, family, and strangers are thinking and always have a good answer. Change the subject. Throw them off the scent (usually by making fun of gay people and talking about some straight experience I didn't have).

By the time I overheard Jeff and Brian talking, all this energy had been packed, unpacked, and repacked to infinity and had finally, finally, reached a Big Bang point. Ha! A homosexual singularity. The faking, pretending, using vague pronouns, lying to my family and friends, never being fully open about the fundamentals of my life and the person living that life—none of that felt normal anymore. These intricate, fragile components of my being exploded in infinite directions on that spring day in 1993.

I lost my normal, my Joanne. And I gained a blank slate to start rewriting my character.

Reflection

If you are not straight . . .

- What do you still carry with you about your childhood experiences?

- What might your current self say to your twelve-year-old self?

- What did you feel when you told that first person you were gay?

- What do you wish could have been different?

- What are you grateful for that you never thought you would be?

- What are you most proud of as a gay person?

If you are straight . . .

- Do you remember kids from your childhood who might have been gay or came out later? How did you treat them?

- What do you think those kids might say about how you treated them?

- What might your current self say to that kid?

- What, if anything, do you wish you might have done differently?

- How did you react the first time someone came out to you?

2

Homophobic Pub Crawlers

First Time Out

Coming Out. Capitalized. Yes, there's the *verbal act* of coming out for the first time, like I did to Jeff and Brian: "I'm gay." Then there's the *process* of coming out. I discuss this more later in the book—that false notion that it's a one-and-done type of thing. For now, I'll note that coming out is much more of a process than straight people imagine, at least after that terrifying and/or empowering act of saying it out loud to someone for the first time.

If someone trusts you enough to tell you they're gay, you represent a moment in time for them. Wherever you fall on their timeline, you're still a point on it, an action item in their action register that supports their overall project plan. They've probably told people before you and will tell people after you. While you may need time to process your reaction to the news, the event is over for you in a few minutes. Meanwhile, the person sharing this information is already anticipating who they'll tell next and when they'll do it.

That project plan helps organize the coming out, given all the others to be told (or not—your call). Here are a few questions to ask yourself when you're embarking on the process of coming out:

- How, when, and in what order will I tell the rest of my key stakeholders?

- What is the risk of them finding out from someone else, and how important is that risk to me?

- If it's important to me, what steps can I take to mitigate that risk?

- How many stakeholder groups are there, and how do I customize the core message for each group?

- What level of information do they need?

- What responses do I have in my toolbox that will help me deal with their reaction?

- How can I maintain control when the situation is impossible to control?

See how time-consuming this process can be? And I haven't even touched on the emotional energy suck that goes with it.

So much planning, timing, and creative messaging: the series of emails (or handwritten letters with postage stamps dropped into a blue mailbox back in my day), difficult conversations and easy ones, decisions about whether to say anything at all—every step out of that closet carries the potential for imagined and real drama.

Once you get through the initial round of *Coming Out*, now you are *Out*. The key milestones have been met. The communications plan is complete. You're now in go-live mode, sustaining the plan. You'll likely come out to more people on an as-needed basis in the future (e.g., that Uber driver who has surprisingly strong opinions about gay marriage), but for now, you've addressed the critical mass. Congratulations. You're out.

"Are you out?" On the face of it, it's a run-of-the-mill, closed-ended question expecting a yes or no response. It comes from someone who already knows you're gay and wants to know who *else* knows it. Back in the mid-nineties (maybe still today?), this question was a great first-date icebreaker because it rarely elicited that simple response. Instead, responses were variations on a theme. "I'm out to friends and coworkers but not to my family," or "Some of my friends know but no one else." My favorite was "What I do with my personal life is no one else's business." Translation: "I'm highly closeted." While I was still coming out but not yet out, I might have used this response once or twice while darting my eyes furtively around the restaurant, hoping no one saw me on a *date with a guy*.

Overall though, once I was out, the walls of those many compartments dissolved into an open floor plan of my life, and I was free at last. The various versions of me finally integrated into a consistent, singular image that no longer required planning which me was on standby for a particular situation.

Besides, I'd already shed most of the old friends who I thought had an issue with me being gay. I didn't make a conscious decision to drop friends on the way to coming out. Most of the time it was thanks to the pink camouflage. People say all sorts of things about other people when they're either 1) sure you agree with their views or 2) don't know you're one of those people. Once I knew Dude X thought so-and-so was acting a little faggoty, or Chick Y was sad to think that gays weren't getting into heaven, I gradually lost interest in sustaining the friendship. Chick Y would have called it a blessing in disguise.

Back to a False Identity

The Village was, and still is, a massive apartment complex in Dallas. Its series of large complexes grouped across dozens of acres in central Dallas forms, well, a village. Each complex has its own pool and its own name—The Green, The Meadow, The Hill, and a few others. In the seventies before equal housing laws were passed, it was THE swinging singles place to live in Dallas. By the time I moved there in the early nineties, the hot tubs had been converted into baby pools. It was still primarily a place for young singles on a tight budget just starting their careers, but the sexual-revolution vibe had faded and been replaced by single fortysomething men who still lived there and nursed drinks alone at the Village Country Club bar.

At five o'clock on the dot every day, I left work and went home to my little one-bedroom apartment in The Green. I was home in time for the six o'clock local news, then *Wheel of Fortune* at six-thirty. I went grocery shopping at Tom Thumb once a week. I met up with friends down on Cedar Springs. If you said Cedar Springs, you meant the gay part of town with all the bars. There was JR's and next door to it, Sue Ellen's, which was the lesbian bar famous for its Thursday-night karaoke. The Roundup was across the street. A country bar where gay cowboys two-stepped to Shania and line-danced to "Achy Breaky Heart," it was where we ended up at the end of the night to play pool and drink gin and tonics. Then the lights came on at two o'clock to close the bar. That's when those who hadn't gotten lucky yet started looking every person in the eyes to see if they looked back, maybe another desperate person who hadn't found someone to go home with and this guy will do in a pinch. My twentysomething friends and I called it "Two O'clock Eyes."

I was out at last and enjoying my freedom. My mom was slowly getting over the news after the fox-guarding-the-henhouse outburst. No one at work seemed to care as much as I had feared.

Strange that at that age, it didn't occur to me that there *could* be real consequences for being gay in Texas, the most benign of which is that we could be fired for simply being gay—we weren't yet a protected class under employment law. Technically, merely existing as a gay person was illegal, but you had to be caught in the act to be considered a criminal. Mercifully, I didn't know this little tidbit at the time, or I might have kept both feet firmly in the closet.

My company didn't fire me. On the contrary, I developed a strong work ethic, worked longer hours, went home to my speck of an apartment, went on dates, got a boyfriend, lost the boyfriend, went to work earlier, received pay increases, drank and shot pool at The Roundup, took on more job responsibilities, dated, got together and broke up some more, got a couple of promotions. When I reflect on it now, I see this young Kevin who looked like he was living a life in that Venn diagram overlapping personal and professional sweet spot. I know that this young adult was desperate to stand out, do things that attracted praise and admiration, and continue to work for others' approval and acceptance. Yeah, all this was exhausting but necessary to keep outperforming others, to keep justifying that Most Likely to Succeed Award from senior year in high school.

When my company offered me a chance to move to the United Kingdom in 1997, it was a gift that I knew would keep on giving approval, acceptance, and admiration. I was going to be an expat! I had visions of meeting the local vicar and becoming great friends as we discussed superintelligent and lofty things. Tons of new friends were already waiting for me and my American accent, no doubt. And my simple act of living abroad was going to impress anyone back in quaint old Texas every time my name came up, which I was sure was going to be often.

On my last day in the office in Dallas, I changed my voice mail message. "Hello. This is Kevin Jones. I've relocated to London, United Kingdom, and am no longer with the Dallas office." I didn't redirect them to someone else. I didn't care. They just needed to know that I was now living in London, UNITED KINGDOM.

If all those callers to my voice mail were impressed, that was nothing compared to how impressed I was with myself. This job transfer entitled me to a business class ticket, a housing allowance, a rental car, and shipping. Shipping! A moving company came and packed up all my stuff for me. No loading my car and a U-Haul. Entering DFW airport on a hot June day in 1997, I flew to London and exited Heathrow into cool breezes and a brand-new future.

Well, almost London, initially anyway. I still had to find a place to live, so in the interim, I was put up in a hotel in Maidenhead, the town west of London where I was going to work. Yes, really. This unfortunate modern English name comes from the riverside area where the first "New wharf" or "Maiden Hythe" in old English was built on the Thames, which flowed through the town on its way to London and out to sea. Still, it elicited ridiculous schoolboy giggles from my friends back in Dallas when I told them where I was staying temporarily. Which was a Holiday Inn. In Maidenhead (tee-hee).

Jet-lagged, I checked in and was presented with a large rectangular piece of plastic with my room number stenciled on it and a real key dangling from it. Real keys. Big metal heavy keys. Ahh, 1997. I took my key and found my room. It had no air conditioning, but it didn't matter because it was the UK in June. The room faced a field that bordered the hotel, so when I opened the window, that amazing fresh, cool air flowed through the room. I was in English-speaking heaven. I could sleep with the windows open. In June. Take *that*, Texas!

There was no coffee maker, just an electric kettle on a tray on the dresser. Next to it was an assortment of teas, sugar, and . . . what the heck . . . little paper tubes of something I'd never seen before. I took a closer look. *Instant coffee*?! These lips have never uttered, "Make mine a cup of Taster's Choice."

I managed to stay awake through the jet lag until some reasonable evening hour, maybe nine o'clock. I don't remember exactly because it was still freaking light outside when I decided to give it up and go to sleep. I had no idea that it stayed light until after ten o'clock that time of year. Despite the light coming through the open window and curtains, it didn't take long to fall asleep. I had a big day tomorrow with my local office orientation. As the cool breezes washed over me, I faded away, thinking of the new life that awaited me the next day.

As birds chirped across the open field, a bright morning sun flooded the cool room with its warming rays. By degrees, my consciousness returned as church bells rang off in the distance. Where was I? I'd woken up in the same position I'd fallen asleep in the night before. Oh yeah. Hotel. England. New life. So idyllic this lovely first morning. The sun seems awfully bright for so early in the morning. Wait . . . Ahhhh shit! *It's not early morning. I'm late for my first day!*

Flying out of bed in a major panic, I ran to the bathroom to turn on the shower, almost passing out from the lightheadedness of jumping up so quickly. As I let the water warm up, I steadied myself on the adorable pedestal sink to regain my balance.

Once the blood returned to my head, I squinted my eyes in deep thought. The thought took shape as it sought the logical part hiding deep within the recesses of my analytical left brain. Hmm. I turned around and left the running water behind me as I stumbled back into the sun-drenched room with its noonday sun. Noonday, my ass, or arse. I looked at the clock on the bedside table—*why hadn't I done that before?* And damned if that clock didn't say 6:03 a.m. Six. Oh. Three. What the hell? Sunrise is six-thirty—everyone knows that! The sun shouldn't even be up yet, much less sending me into a huge lightheaded freak-out, with its warming rays and golden beams caressing the room in a blazing glow of glory. I looked again. 6:04 a.m. Orientation started at nine-thirty—three effing hours from now. Oh well, I was up and nowhere close to being able to fall back asleep again. Later, I'd learn that at this time of year, being so far north, sunrise was some crazy-ass time like 4:45 a.m., so of course by six, it feels like the middle of the day.

With Foreign Country Living Lesson One complete, I returned to the bathroom with the kettle from the tea tray, turned off the shower, and filled the kettle at the sink. Once the water boiled, I helped myself to a steaming cup of instant coffee (don't get me started, it's only 6:09 a.m.).

****

I managed to make it to the office for orientation, where I met my peer buddy, Julian. Julian was a ridiculously tall cricket player. He had the good fortune of taking me around the floor and introducing me to my new teammates. I followed him in the long shadow he cast as we moved from desk to desk, kitchen to mail room. We chatted with each person, asking and answering questions to make conversation. *Where in the US was I from? Oh, Texas. Where are your cowboy boots, ha ha.* We moved around the office, meeting one male after another. Out of about twenty people on the team I met that day, all but one, Sue, was male. It didn't take long for me to notice how this impacted the culture of the group. Bragging about their sexual accomplishments over the weekend, which of the women who worked at the firm had nice tits or asses, who could out-drink whom, and so on. And in case you're wondering, after orientation, the HR person had disappeared, never to be seen again.

I settled in amongst the jokes and teasing—mostly sexual, off-color, or lighthearted kidding. But then there was an afternoon that confirmed a creeping suspicion. While I was working at my big, bulky computer, a handful of guys were talking a few feet away in the hallway.

They were teasing one of the younger guys about his lack of progress in getting his girlfriend to do more with him in bed. They gave him all sorts of terrible—and sometimes impossible—advice, with each piece receiving a round of laughter.

The conversation grew more explicit as I waited for the inevitable question. And then there it was. Was he gay? No, he swore, he was no poof, *they* were. Since they seemed so curious about his sex life and body parts, it all made sense now. *They* must be *that way*. No other explanation for it. "Who wants to pop into the loo with me to see how lucky my girlfriend is?" At that, they all burst out laughing as I stared blankly at the data on my screen about cell phone penetration rates in Russia and had a flashback to junior high. *Keithy! There you ARE, you silly boy! What are you doing after school today? Want to come over to my place? Hey, faggot, we're talking to you. Are you gay? Where's your boyfriend? Maybe he'll pick up your books.*

A few days later, Julian and I were having lunch with a few coworkers. By this point, I could tell Julian wasn't a big Kevin fan, but he was my peer buddy for the entire first month, so he *had* to be nice to me. I couldn't put my finger on it, though I had my suspicions about his suspicions; the friendship chemistry just wasn't there. Some chatter to pass the time was underway when Damien asked me why I had moved to the UK. I was giving some sort of answer about new adventure, culture, new people—something like that— when I saw a twinkle in his eye. I talked a bit longer, becoming more aware of something shared wordlessly with the others around the table.

"I'm going to stop you right there," he said. "We've been talking about you and we're certain we know more about you than you're letting on."

I laughed nervously, protesting that I was sure I didn't know what they were talking about.

"Something happened back in Dallas, didn't it?" he asked. "You broke up with your girlfriend and thought you'd make a new start here. With that American accent, you figured you could pull any girl you wanted, isn't that right, mate? Well, I've got good news. She's going to kill us for letting you know, but she—and you—will both thank us later. Sue fancies you. After lunch, go on over and ask her out."

Everyone at the table burst into laughter. And so did I. They'd caught me. Boy, they'd caught me. They figured me out. The game was up. And they were going to help me get back in the saddle with a new girl after that heart-wrenching breakup way back in Texas. All I needed was a new girl in my life, and I'd be right as rain. And what was even better, she was right here in the office so they could all watch as the new romance unfolded. Yay! I was a straight guy starting over in a new country after a nasty breakup. I was going to ask Sue out.

And with that, I switched to survival mode and headed back into the closet.

Escape from the Homophobic Hole

A quarter of a century. That's how long it's been since that lunch, though it might have been an hour ago. My flushed face, the pounding in my chest, the panic of not knowing what to do next are all still vivid, not the mention the terror of thinking of going on a date with a girl and how *that* evening might end.

Fortunately, that evening never started. Turns out Sue thought I was a nice guy, but she wasn't interested in going on a date. She was on-again, off-again seeing someone and didn't think going out with a guy from the office was a great idea. Whew! Though if I'd been straight, I might have fancied her, as they say over there.

After this incident, there were two things I knew for sure: 1) I couldn't—didn't want to—deal with this sort of crap again, and 2) these guys were wankers. Fortunately, I'd chosen to live in London while our office was just far enough west of London to make hanging out too often a logistical challenge, given the traffic and unreliability of the trains back then. Darn. But I still went out for a pint or two after work in the Maidenhead High Street.

My flat—such a cool word to this Southeast Texas boy—was on the top floor of an old Edwardian house. Like the majority of the Georgian, Victorian, and Edwardian houses in London, each of the four floors had been converted into flats by the owners years ago. After a few weeks as a guest at the Holiday Inn Maidenhead, I found the perfect place to live in West London. No elevator—just an old converted house with lots of stairs. And a roof terrace! But no dishwasher. Or dryer. But it had a *roof terrace*. I spent many beautiful evenings up there during that summer of 1997, when the UK was experiencing drought conditions. I watched the late sunsets over the Novotel in Hammersmith while the Concorde roared overhead as it glided majestically toward Heathrow. Evening breezes from every direction up there on that roof cooled me into disbelief that I might be chilly in July. It was all so, so *magical*.

And it was there, in that flat, in Baron's Court in West London, that I was gay. At the same time that I was straight in Maidenhead. I was leading a double life. I bought a car, learned to drive on the other side of the road, and drove out to the Maidenhead Office Park—MOP for short—every day for the next couple of years. The after-work pints with coworkers grew less frequent. And what a relief. You can't go out with people after work and not talk at least a little about your life outside of work. And that was getting harder because I was openly gay in London. The more open my life there became, the more cautiously I chose my words in Maidenhead, to the point that I not only politely declined the offers to head to the local pub after work, but I also interacted less with the guys during work.

I think back on that first experience with self-selecting out. I increasingly kept to myself. In a performance review, I learned that I wasn't thought of as a team player. I didn't have the courage to ask my manager what he meant by that, but I knew. I wasn't one of the guys anymore. When promotion time came around, I met all the criteria for experience, ratings, and the other professional boxes that needed to be checked. But the promotion didn't come through. I just wasn't "quite there yet," in the words of my manager. I was angry and confused, and that time, I found the courage to ask for examples. And wouldn't you know, he couldn't give me one. Not being "quite there yet," I asked what I could do in the coming year to get there and received the super-helpful advice to just keep doing what I was doing. I was being quietly fired before quiet firing was cool.

An alternate reality plays in my head sometimes in which I say something like, "Bugger off, mates, I'm gay," and accept the professional consequences of being labeled the office poofter from there on out. And I know for sure that this is how my corporate life would have played out back then while I waited for time, culture, and perceptions to change. I still wouldn't have been promoted, but who knows? What if they ended up not caring about my sexuality as much as I imagined and laughed it off as I accepted the next invitation to join them at the pub? What if my image shifted into one of a solid team player now that I was hanging out with the lads after work again? Maybe I could have gotten that promotion.

An exercise in futility, maybe—the past is the past. Except that when we talk about gay people and where they are in their careers now, these are the same people who were in their twenties then. We had to make all sorts of decisions about whom to tell and trust, how coming out might affect our daily lives (forget careers, what would it be like just getting through each day?), and whether to go along with the laughter and jokes about gay people or proudly announce who we really were. Every time we were told we weren't a team player, that we weren't quite there yet, or whatever bullshit was code for "you're different even if we can't say exactly why," it reinforced the infinite number of microdecisions we were making about our careers that straight people have never needed to consider. And for many of us, the result of those accumulated decisions over time was a career ladder that was much harder to climb, or at least not as quickly or as directly as our straight peers.

But back to the MOP for a moment. After not getting the promotion, I knew my career trajectory was hurtling unfettered toward a discriminatory dead end. I could stay in the closet and continue to be labeled a bad team player. Or I could come out and take my chances, which didn't look very good considering there were no gay people at the company in the UK office—at least not openly so. Neither of those options, I was certain, was going to be the catalyst for a flourishing career. Unfortunately, my work visa was tied to my employer, so looking for a position elsewhere in the UK wasn't an option. I could return to the US, suck it up and stay where I was for the Good Lord only knows how long, or find a third as yet undetermined miracle option.

And lo and behold, a miracle of sorts emerged from Berkeley Square, right in the heart of London.

After two years at the MOP, I still was unaware we had an office in London. It housed people in functions that required proximity to resources in London, like our legal group, certain sales groups that supported large clients there, and our government affairs group. And after a couple of months of increasingly desperate searches of our internal, primitive, early-intranet job site, the miracle occurred, and I rejoiced: an open position in Government Affairs glowed back at me from the cathode-ray tube of my desktop monitor.

I applied, received an offer for a first-round interview, made it past that first round, and found myself preparing for a second interview with the UK head of the group. Richard was a former diplomat and intelligence officer with the UK government, recruited directly out of Oxford in the sixties. A typical and cozy setup between Oxford, Cambridge, and the government at the time, but so alien to me and my Texas world back home. As I prepared for the interview with Richard, I knew for damn sure that it was going to be different this time, if I got the job. And whether I got the job or not, I was going to be up front, *during the interview*, about my sexuality. And if I didn't get the job for whatever reason, I'd pack up and head back to the States. What a freaking liberating decision!

The interview had been going well. And did I mention I loved the commute—six stops on the Tube from my flat to the office? No stupid drive away from this amazing city out to the MOP and a bunch of wankers. Richard didn't care that I didn't have formal government affairs experience. I was so junior at that point it wasn't expected—I could learn the ropes from him and the other more senior people in the group. He was intrigued with the idea of having an American in this type of role in the UK. Then, as we neared the end of the interview, he asked if I had any questions for him. I don't remember the exact words, but I remember the adrenaline rush as I told him I was gay and said that if it mattered, I'd prefer he tell me now.

Richard was a marvelous old-school Brit. He was old enough to have worn a bowler hat before such outward symbols of the British class system faded away for good in the seventies. He remembered the bland postwar ration years when one simply made do with what one had. And typically, his facial expressions rarely betrayed what he was thinking.

So when I made my bold request, he disappointed me in that, aside from a slight twitch of a primordial smile at the distant edges of his mouth, he gave me nothing to go on. Then he cleared his throat, looked at me as a smile spread across his face, and said, "Oh, there were plenty of homosexuals at Oxford and, I think you'll find, plenty in government."

***

Twenty-five years. It's easy to pass it off as a different time with different attitudes. That's still how I think about my experience in Maidenhead because I'd like to think that when we look back in another quarter century, we'll be pleased with how much more progress we've made in our DEI efforts without passing judgment on our past collective selves.

Richard has passed away. I could look up the others I ended up working with in Government Affairs, but I haven't. They were older than me, and indeed, I did learn quite a lot from them, just as Richard said I would. No one cared that I was gay, or if they did, they didn't let it show. That switch, finally crawling out of that homophobic hole, wasn't quite as brave as coming out to Jeff and Brian back in Dallas, though it was the most deliberate, planned act of coming out in my career. Even now, I look back on that nerve-wracking yet determined act as a major milestone in my career. I started that new role as a gay man on the very first day and never looked inside another corporate closet again.

I don't know for sure, but I want to believe those guys out in Maidenhead have evolved in their thinking over these years, in how they view themselves and others, just as I have. If reminded of that day when they were so sure I'd gone through a breakup with a woman and needed to jump back on the horse, maybe they'd even be horrified now at the assumptions they made, knowing how it affected me. It's possible they don't even remember it. On the other hand, I'll wager that they are *the same* as they were then. I'll bet they're still wankers.

Reflection

If you are not straight . . .

- What was your life like before you came out?

- And you were closeted at work, what do you remember about that time?

- And you are closeted at work today, what are the reasons you're closeted? What do you want others to understand about those reasons?

- And you are out at work now, what difference has it made to your professional life?

- How has being out—or closeted—affected how you manage your performance at work?

- How many times do you estimate that you have come out?

If you are straight . . .

- How might your professional life differ from a gay person's?

- And you knew someone at work was gay and closeted, would you say anything to them? If so, what? If not, why not?

- What do you want a gay person to know about you?

- What part of yourself might you feel uncomfortable about revealing to a gay person?

3

Blowing the Closet Door Off

Meet Simon, My Love

St. Bride's is one of the most stunning churches in London. A St. Bride's has stood on this site since roughly the seventh century, though the current one is only a few hundred years old, having been designed by Sir Christopher Wren following the Great Fire of London in 1666. Only a few *hundred* years old.

In September 2000, I had the beautiful honor of being part of my friends Janie and Dave's wedding in this magnificent church, whose bell tower looks like the tiers of a wedding cake. And I can tell you that this Texan felt quite English, dressed in my morning suit and hand-embroidered waistcoat and vest. Straight out of *Four Weddings and a Funeral.*

Standing in that beautiful church, autumnal morning sun blazing through the windows as a beautiful Janie walked down the nave to Delibes' "The Flower Duet," I looked uh-mazing on the outside. Inside, my emotions weren't having it, choosing to throw a raucous pity party instead. *Why don't I have someone in my life? I deserve someone. I'm finally out—I'm out everywhere, dang it. I'm a catch. I hate this city; it's too big to meet anyone normal.*

Yeah, London. Hated it. Where all my other friends had met, broken up, met, hooked up, shacked up, cohabitated, or were married by this point. I was the guy Samuel Johnson spoke about when he said, " . . . when a man is tired of London, he is tired of life; for there is in London all that life can afford."

Poor me. I was all alone. London was solely to blame for my solitary life, a life destined for the gay equivalent of Barry Manilow's Lola the Showgirl, propped up at a gay West End bar every night for the rest of my life, bumming cigarettes and telling stories of how fabulous I looked that day in September back in 2000.

But that vision of a tragic, solitary life was shattered exactly one week later, when I met this brown-eyed, dimpled-faced secondary school teacher from Winchester named Simon. We hit it off immediately at the bar, so I asked him out on a date. He stammered a bit as he explained that he was accompanying his students on a trip to France and was unavailable for a couple of weeks. *Of course, figures. Just say you're not interested.*

We continued talking and exchanged phone numbers, and I prepared for the slow ghosting game—the one where you call each other once, hoping for the answering machine. *What relief—got the answering machine.* Leave a message, they do the same thing, and that's that. I go back to my tragic life of faded feathers in my hair and a dress cut down to there.

Except this guy had other plans. He *did* go off to France with his school kids. And from there, he sent me a postcard of the Bayeux Tapestry. I pulled it out of the mailbox of my old Edwardian house/flat conversion, overcome by relief that he wasn't an immediate flake and simultaneously a bit alarmed that he had my address.

When he returned, he called me, I answered, we chatted, agreed to go on a date, and then *did*. I met him after work on the steps of St. Martin-in-the-Fields, a church just on the eastern side of Trafalgar Square. Such a strange thing to think about all these years later. We made plans and agreed on a time we'd meet. We provided no updates via text on our exact location or ETA. We just arranged to do something, then showed up at the agreed-upon time.

I held my umbrella low as I turned the corner into the onslaught of horizontal rain that had soaked me from the knees down and saw Simon standing on the porch of that beautiful church, sheltering from the typical British fall weather. We had Tex-Mex for dinner. Yes, I know. Tex-Mex in London—I was quite the sophisticate. We went to a movie, *Oh Brother, Where Art Thou?* We had more dates. Someone said I love you first, and the other said it back.

And I began referring to him at work. I didn't talk about vague events that happened the previous weekend in my new role. I said that Simon and I did this and that. Or a funny thing happened to *me and Simon*. I'd love to say that it came naturally, but that was far from the case at first. I found the courage to ditch the vague "they" pronoun and replaced it with a live person's name and matching pronoun.

Those first few times, I hunted meticulously for a facial twitch, a change in the way a coworker looked at me, a change in the way they looked at each other, anything that might betray their true homophobic selves when I mentioned Simon's name. I came up short every time, and eventually, I stopped looking.

It felt great, though it was more profound than that. I felt at ease. No longer guarded. Not making decisions by the millisecond about what to say or hold back during a work conversation. For the first time, I was out, not leaving parts of me behind in my flat as I left to catch the Tube each day for work. That whole self took the Tube, walked to the office, did his work, chatted with colleagues, went out for drinks after work, and went back home the same person he was when he left. The same whole person.

Meanwhile, Simon was still living a different sort of life.

I Love They—Actually He

Simon was a high school teacher in Winchester. If you think teachers don't make much money here, try living on their UK salary. Maybe it's changed in the twenty-plus years since then, but not likely.

He rented a room from a couple because it was all he could afford. He wasn't out to them. He wasn't out at school. He wasn't out to his family. He was solidly inside the closet behind a padlocked door. He took the train from Winchester on the occasional weekend evening to go out and be himself in London, which is fortunate for me since that's how we met.

Most weekends, he hopped on the train a closeted man in Winchester and arrived at London Waterloo sort of out. From there, he located one of those iconic red phone boxes that were still ubiquitous in late 2000 and early 2001 and called me at my flat in Baron's Court. He was either telling me that he had arrived and was about to take the Tube to me or we were discussing where I'd take the Tube to meet him. This became our weekly Friday through Sunday routine once we started dating. From Friday evening to Sunday afternoon, he brought his entire self to life. He met my friends. We all went out. They knew us as a couple. Then on Sunday afternoons, he caught the train back to Winchester. On that hour-long ride, he gently eased back into the closet and closed the door.

We talked on the phone during the week. The couple Simon rented his room from had one phone in the house, which I soon learned was in the hallway. Usually, he called me before I got the chance to call him, though occasionally I'd reach him first. When I did, sometimes one of the owners answered, and I would ask for Simon. Then I'd wait in silence while they went to get him or call out to him.

Sometimes Simon sounded a little off, stilted, *formal*. I was a little slow on the uptake because it took quite a few times of hearing that distant-sounding voice before I connected the dots that whenever he sounded like that, someone else was in the house and could hear him. Someone who didn't know he was gay. Someone who, if he spoke in his normal voice, would just absolutely, without a doubt, figure out in a heartbeat that he was a big ole flaming English queen.

He made sure they knew that I was an old friend from London. I doubt they cared, but that was our story. I don't think he ever explained the American accent. But once that turned into our routine, it became fun. For me. When they answered, I'd introduce myself as Simon's old friend from London and ask if he was around. Or exaggerate my southern accent so that "hi" became "hiiiiiiiii," as in, "Hiiiiii, is Simon thay-uuuuure?" Oh, what fun we had indeed.

The fun ended when he finally got a cell phone, darn it. But he stayed in the closet.

His problem was that while being gay wasn't against the rules for a high school teacher, it could easily have made things difficult for him. Imagine a kid being angry at a teacher. Knowing the teacher is gay, what might that kid do? Let your mind go to the darkest places. It's not hard. Look around at what's happening in our schools today, where even talking about being LGBTQ+ is considered "grooming." He was a high school teacher in an ancient but provincial town an hour's train ride from London, and he didn't want to take any chances.

His mum was different. Mums always are. He doesn't remember when, but at some point after we started dating, she asked why he went up to London every weekend. He made up something about Winchester being boring, that there were museums—*museums!*—in London that he enjoyed, friends who lived there, and so on. We know now she wasn't buying it, but she let it go. The more he referred to me as "they" or "them," the less he mentioned a singular friend as a "he" or "she" back in the day when those were the only options, the more she suspected something was up. Unfortunately, they were British, so when the conversation grew uncomfortable, someone inevitably brought up the weather.

I didn't care. I really didn't. I knew exactly what it was like—where Simon was, what he was experiencing with the carefully chosen pronouns. Yes, referring to someone as "they" is awkward at both ends of the conversation. The person listening usually wants to ask more but instinctively knows not to. The person speaking desperately wants the person not to ask more and quickly moves the conversation along so they can't.

It was his choice, his time, his comfort level. That comfort level started dropping, and from that drop, he found the courage to tell his sister he was gay. I met her. We were all cool with it. She loved me (of course), and we had a wonderful time. That gave way to finally telling his mother—my now mother-in-law—and the floodgates opened for him to be who he fully was, not just in London but in Winchester and Devon too.

Precious little story. But what does a gay guy coming out in the South of England have to do with bias in corporate America? It's the very existence of bias that makes us use vague pronouns to start with. In corporate America, it's the reason many people still aren't out. Far from using "they" as a pronoun to refer to friends or acquaintances who identify with it, it's used in anticipation of that bias in the workplace. We *know* it's there. That one little pronoun—referring to the person we love more than anyone else in the world—enables a deliberate vagueness so we can control the narrative. We're used to doing it. "They" doesn't sound quite right, but it's not quite wrong enough to question. We control what you know about our personal lives. "They" gives us a way of talking about what we did over the weekend and with whom without telling you who we are.

If we can even get comfortable with a vague pronoun. More likely, we become pros at decision diamonds and deflecting. This image, adapted from Claudia Brind-Woody's "The Cost of Thinking Twice," sums up what many a gay person has gone through at the water cooler.[1]

---

[1] Claudia Brind-Woody, "The Cost of Thinking Twice," Presentation from Nykredit's LGBT-conference in Copenhagen, August 23, 2013, The cost of thinking twice by Claudia Brind-Woody 08-23-13 (slideshare.net).

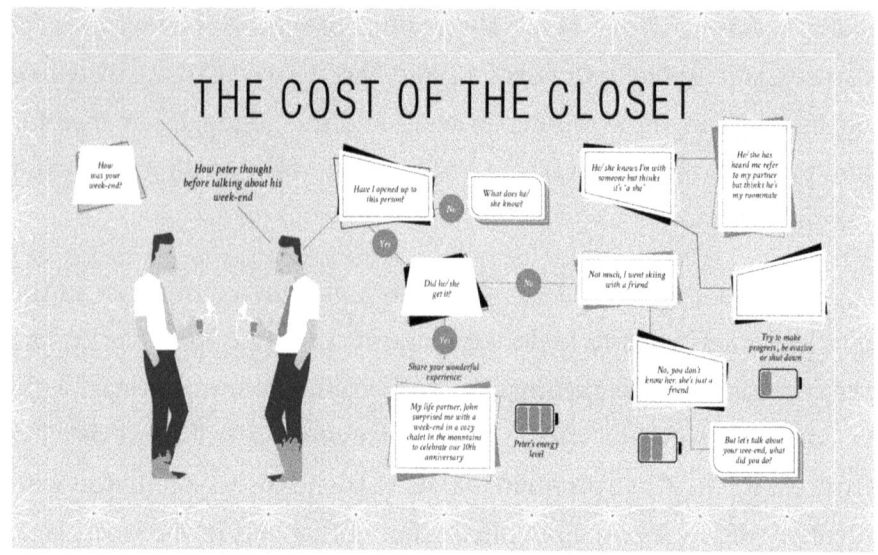

THE COST OF THE CLOSET

Man, that's some level of stress! Poor Peter. No big surprise he's got only one bar of juice left by the end of that conversation. One conversation. It's tiring. Stressful. Risky. Never mind that Peter is making these decisions within microseconds, he's likely also feeling a slew of other emotions that he's grown good at suppressing: Guilt: *I hate that I'm betraying John by referring to him as a "friend" and a "her."* Confusion: *Is this the guy who knows I'm with someone and thinks it's a "she," or am I mixing him up with someone else?* It gets tough keeping all those stories straight, excuse the pun. Anxiety: *When can I flip this conversation around to his weekend without it seeming awkward or suspicious?* Desperation: *How can I get out of this conversation before I reveal too much?*

And no, Peter isn't overthinking this conversation. The *Harvard Business Review*'s research on work-family conflict in organizations assumed that employees belong to a heterosexual family structure. They wanted to determine whether previous similar studies applied in a similar way to lesbian, gay, or bisexual (LGB) employees and their families. They interviewed 53 LGB employees in the US across various industries and job types. In the study, they asked the interviewees about their work-family experiences at their current organizations. Not surprisingly, they found that LGB employees experience similar work-family conflicts as their heterosexual counterparts. But what they also uncovered is that LGB employees deal with additional conflicts that don't affect their straight colleagues:

> [M]ost of the people in our sample were out about their personal sexual orientation at work. In other words, their coworkers knew that they were lesbian, gay, or bisexual, but they still didn't always feel confident that bringing their partner to events was a good idea. Many felt that having their family "on display" ran the risk of their coworkers thinking that they were trying to make a political statement or attempting to be too brazen about their sexual orientation in the workplace.[2]

And this is coming from the people who are already out. Imagine if you're Peter and you're selectively out. This is advanced stuff for him. In effect, even when they're out, there's a worry about whether their colleagues see them as knowing their place. They're out, but their family is "on display." Not something you typically think about when you see a heterosexual family. It's just there. Separate and unequal.

---

[2] Katina Sawyer, Christian N. Thoroughgood, and Jamie J. Ladge, "How Companies Make It Harder for Lesbian, Gay, and Bisexual Employees to Achieve Work-Life Balance," *Harvard Business Review,* August 23, 2018, How Companies Make It Harder for Lesbian, Gay, and Bisexual Employees to Achieve Work-Life Balance (hbr.org).

Look back at Peter's decision diamond about having opened up to this person. He's got a lot of decisions to make before he decides the "right" narrative for his ski trip. He's careful, calculated, wary. The Harvard Study provides a poignant example of how these decision diamonds play out across the country:

> [E]mployees also dealt with these conflicts by being careful about which family issues they talked about at work, and with whom. This meant that many had to evaluate who was "safe" and who was "questionable," weighing the risks of opening up. One participant noted, "Where I work isn't accepting of alternative lifestyles, so I don't talk about family other than my children. I don't talk about my partner except with a few people I trust."[3]

For us gay folks, none of this is surprising research. We've lived and breathed it, this two-phased approach to coming out:

- Decision Diamond 1: Do I come out to Person A? Yes/No

- Decision Diamond 2: Do I tell Person A, whom I've come out to, about X*? Yes/No

  *Where X = spouse, home life, trips, social events, friends, children/children's activities, and benign references to being woken up by spouse's snoring (is that too sexual for Person A? I mean, I know there's no reference to sex, but what would they think if they start to visualize us in the same bed because I said my spouse snores? Would they picture us having sex? I don't want to picture *them* having sex when they talk about *their* spouse snoring).

---

[3] Sawyer, "How Companies."

In effect, there's the *theory* and the *practice*. Theory says, "I understand that you're gay." Practice says, "I know details about you as a gay person." That intersection between theory and practice at the organizational level is what makes all the Peters out there nervous wrecks. I can know you're gay and not care. Once you start revealing additional information that wraps around that gay nugget, I either accept each new piece, or I feel like you're shoving your lifestyle down my throat.

As the gay person, I run each comment, phrase, and thought with even a tangential connection to my sexuality through multiple filters. I decide whether to share that information, to accept the risk that I might be judged for it. The other person decides whether it's information they want to hear and acts accordingly based on their beliefs and values about homosexuality. *They won't like me now. What if they talk about me behind my back? Will they call me names? Will they make a funny face?* The reactions are more subtle now, but it's still seventh grade in that groovy mid-century building all over again.

Reflection

If you are not straight . . .

- What do you remember about your first nonheterosexual date?

- Did you talk about that first date at work? Why or why not?

- What was it like to socialize with other nonstraight people for the first time?

- What do you recall about an early conversation you had with a straight coworker?

If you are straight . . .

- How might your memories of your first date differ from those of someone who isn't straight?

- Do you talk to your coworkers about your dates or your partner?

- What was it like to socialize with a gay person for the first time?

- What do you remember about an early conversation you had with a gay coworker?

4

Back in the USA

Visa Interview

First, loft apartments in Dallas—the authentic kind converted from old warehouses—have air conditioning systems that make you feel like you're lying underneath an old Concorde as it takes off. So freaking loud. That part was not mentioned in the ad when I was looking online for places to live when we were planning to move back to the US. I saw "concrete floors and exposed brick walls," a novel concept for Dallas at a time when millennials were nursing sippy cups of milk instead of iced lattes. The air conditioning ductwork was suspended from the ceiling by wires and consisted of metal tubes with slatted vents cut open at intervals. Each cycle, just before it turned on, consisted of a sucking whoosh followed by the roar of icy air blasting out of those slats. All day, every day, from April to October.

So there I was in bed on a June night, sleeping and waking through the sucking and blowing and whooshing and rattling, with my early-model Nokia cell phone on full volume so I wouldn't miss the call from Simon. He was at the US embassy back in London, scheduled for a ten-thirty a.m. interview—the final step to obtaining his F-1 student visa.

Around four in the morning, or ten a.m. London time, when he was emptying his pockets to go through security and smiling cautiously at the machine-gun-toting marine at the metal detector, I said, "To hell with it," and got out of bed for good. The freaking air conditioning was doing its thing, and so was my mind. This was the last step in a long bureaucratic process. We'd followed every step to the letter. There was no logical reason he'd be turned down. Logic at four in the morning, however, is a bit of a rebel; it doesn't follow the stinking rules.

I got up, made a cup of coffee, and opened a pack of Marlboro Lights. Yes, yes, superbad for me, and I don't smoke now, but damn, I needed that cigarette in the itty-bitty hours of that morning as my mind raced through infinite what-ifs. What if the government had done some sort of background check and discovered we were living together, figured it all out, and was waiting for my innocent, nervous Simon to walk into their trap in Grosvenor Square? Had we missed a step? What if we had and didn't know it, and we'd have to start again from scratch? The only what-if I didn't want to think about as I inhaled was what if they turned him down?

***

In 2004, around the time Simon and I took our first steps toward moving back to the US, Marcia Kadish and Tanya McCloskey had become the first legally married same-sex couple in the US. Mind you, their marriage was recognized only in Massachusetts. Following the passage of the Defense of Marriage Act in 1996, twenty-five states had banned same-sex marriage, with the count continuing its climb in the years following. Ohio and Oregon were in the middle of banning it about the time Simon was having his university credentials translated into the American system as part of his visa application.

Because we weren't married, which is to say because we weren't *allowed* to marry, Simon couldn't accompany me on the move back to the US, based on our relationship. If anything, I was acutely suspicious of the US government knowing anything at all about our connection to each other as we began the process of applying for a student visa for him. The full bureaucratic process is too tedious to recount, though the key aspects of applying to a university, translating his credentials, and taking the Graduate Record Exam (GRE) were all prerequisites to even starting to apply for the visa itself.

Once Simon started that part, a critical requirement was proving that he had sufficient funds to support himself while he was a student in the US. He could do it easily enough by presenting a bank statement showing a balance in the tens of thousands of dollars that had been held in the account for at least a year. In our case, we had that money. The only problem here was that it was in a joint account. *"Who is Kevin Jones, and why do you have a joint account with him?"* they might ask. *Application rejected!* With more than half the states having banned same-sex marriage, no, I don't believe I was overreacting to the possibility. So with the help of my sister and brother-in-law, we came up with a Plan B.

If you couldn't prove you had the funds to support yourself, the application gave you the option of having someone in the US sponsor you financially during your time there. All you needed was a notarized letter from your sponsor with copies of their bank statements. So my sister and brother-in-law wrote the letter and provided the required documentation and information. They weren't really going to pay for Simon to live in the US because we were fine on our own. Though if push came to shove, by God, I'd transfer money to them periodically that they would give to him to keep the paper trail clean. Anything to keep the government from establishing a connection between the two of us to keep us apart.

Thinking about it all these years later, maybe I was a tad paranoid. While financially there was no issue with me being able to support Simon here in the US when we moved back, I didn't want the government to know there was any linkage between him and me, fearful that our relationship alone might be enough to reject his visa. So ridiculous. The likelihood of the US government digging into the minutiae of private lives seems so far-fetched. And yet lately, it also doesn't.

Anyway, Simon crushed the GRE. His UK university credentials were duly translated. He applied to Southern Methodist University's Master of Education program and was accepted. He received the offer letter, a crucial step among an infinite number of steps in an infinitely intricate process. The last big push was the embassy interview.

Meanwhile, I wasn't sitting still. I was looking for jobs back in the US on Monster.com and submitting résumés. I was in a career that I didn't really like, where ancient Lords ran their feet up my trousered leg at luncheons in Parliament and where no one offered up unique perspectives about current affairs before asking others for theirs, then adopting that one as their own. I was ready to start over—new country, new career, whatever I needed to do so Simon and I could be together back in the US. Not sure why I'd grown so homesick. We were living in the UK and had a wonderful life. My grandmother had passed away the year before, and my nieces and nephews were growing older without me in their lives, so there was that. Knowing what I know now, I wonder if I would have made a different decision, but that's irrelevant nearly twenty years and a lot of gray hair later.

Finally, I found an opening at Ernst & Young (EY). I called an old friend who used to work there, and her sleuthing revealed that the hiring manager had been in her EY Bible study group. My friend contacted her, put in a good word, and I got an interview. Simon and I had already decided, in the first of many chances we'd take on this journey, that I'd move back to Texas once everything except the embassy appointment was set. Bear in mind, this was way before Zoom or Teams or Slack or whatever, so while an expectation of getting a first phone interview was reasonable, getting a second or third round, much less receiving an offer via phone, sight unseen, was not.

So I made and froze lasagna, cookie dough, and all sorts of other things that Simon could bake or reheat after I left. I packed a couple of suitcases, leaving most of my things at our little house in the London suburbs, since I planned on coming back to help Simon with the final move. And with that assumption, there were no sad goodbyes. I took a taxi to the train station, hopped on a train that took me eventually to Heathrow, and lifted off westward-bound for Dallas.

I got the job at EY. I told them I'd be happy to start in a couple of months. They told me they'd be more than happy for me to start in two weeks. So much for going back to the UK to help Simon with the final move. He'd be on his own for that too, if we made it that far.

***

I lit another cigarette and looked at that old phone. It was 5:23 a.m., a full fifty-three minutes after his interview started. It must have ended by now. Four-thirty was when my brain really had gone full throttle, so by now, I was drinking coffee and chain-smoking like I was in a sixties-era NYC diner. Then the phone rang. "Unknown caller." You got that in the past when it was a non-domestic number that the cell network didn't recognize. I clicked the green button on the top right of the keypad and said hello.

Though of course it was Simon, his voice was strained. Or stressed. It's tough to remember exactly what it sounded like now other than distinctly not his usual voice. Not like anything I'd heard before. He was calling from his cell phone, and given the exorbitant rates charged back then for international calling, he had to be quick. He told me that he had arrived at the American Embassy and checked in for his appointment, the uneasiness growing as he waited to tell the interviewer our little white lie. After a while, his name was called, he went to the desk, and was directed to an office down the hall. As he walked down the hall, he knew this wasn't going to work. What level of crime was he committing? Will they let him call me before they haul him off to jail?

He walked into the office and shook hands with his interviewer, who, pleasantly enough, asked him to sit down while she reviewed his paperwork. Behind her was a glass wall that revealed a corridor separating a row of glass-encased offices on the other side of it. And her office had a door that opened onto the corridor, like a mid-century glass-enclosed version of a secret passage in an old castle.

Anyway, she asked him basic questions about where he was going to study, why he wanted to go to the US, what did he think Texas

64

was going to be like—softball questions like that. Then, "Why would people you appear to barely know want to sponsor you financially?" There it was. He knew it was going to be a question. We'd practiced his response. It wasn't all a lie: my sister and brother-in-law at that point *did* know him, barely, but they knew how much he meant to me. And if it had gotten right down to it, they would have paid his way. It was all so ridiculous, this charade of finances, simply because there was no path to go to the US at the time solely based on our relationship.

He answered as we discussed. His American friend (that's me!) introduced him to his sister and brother-in-law several months ago. Once he'd decided to pursue his master's in the US, he knew he needed financial sponsorship. He talked about it with his friend (me again!), who suggested that these relatives would love to help. He connected them, they talked on the phone about the financial commitment, they had been more than blessed financially, and if it was God's will to help someone who wanted to come to the US, then they wanted to help carry out his will. That last part, while not untrue, since my sister and brother-in-law are the most amazing examples of people who abide by the principles of their faith, was not exactly how the conversation went. It was just a nice little shot of Americana for the good folks at the US Embassy.

The interviewer read the signed document from them. She looked at Simon. He looked back at her, eyes darting from her left eye to her right eye and back, knowing he looked suspicious while she sensed fear.

She pushed her chair back from her desk and asked him to wait there. She opened the door and crossed the transparent hallway to the office opposite. He saw her speaking to another woman who, after a few moments, glanced over at him. She looked back at the papers his interviewer held in her hand. They spoke some more. Then the interviewer crossed back across to her office, to Simon. She asked him to return to the waiting area so that she could discuss his application further with her supervisor. Well, that couldn't be good, could it?

His face felt hot as he left her office and went back out to a busy open space with rows of chairs. Staring at the big clock on the wall, he watched each minute tick by, wondering how long it took for the paperwork for his arrest to be drawn up. Didn't seem like it should take this long. Maybe they had to wait for the London police to show up?

After a while, the interviewer came down the hall and asked him to come back to her office. Once in there, she closed the door, asked him to sit down while she stood, and told him that she didn't believe his story. There it was—what he'd been afraid of was finally happening. Now for the punishment phase.

"While I don't believe you, I don't have a good reason to deny your request since everything is in order. I'm making a note that I don't believe you, but your visa request has been approved." I remember every one of these words as he relayed them to me.

This entire replay of his experience took less than five minutes. His voice quivered. I knew he'd been crying a bit. He'd waited to collect himself before calling me. But we had the visa! I played up the positive outcome, telling him repeatedly how happy and proud I was of him for having the courage to see this through all because of our relationship. But now he had to get going. The call was expensive, and he had to catch his train. We'd talk later that evening when I got home.

I pushed the disconnect button on my phone about the same time as my face grew red with anger. Fuck this! The only reason we had to do this was because we were gay and couldn't get married, and the US only allowed this kind of visa for spouses. Well hell, if you'd let us get married, then he'd be my spouse. This was such a ridiculous catch-22! I don't mean to curse here, but the Kevin back then smoked and cursed, so you know, authenticity of the story and all that.

Poor Simon. I hated this whole shitteree, as a relative used to call a clusterfuck. He was on the receiving end of the US government's skepticism, all because we wanted to start a life back in my home country, which I wasn't too fond of. As I write this over seventeen years later, it still makes me angry. Yes, a lot has changed, and we're married now. And I'm grateful for every up and down and challenge and opportunity we've had together, but this one was so unnecessarily banal.

But the US government approved the visa. I decided to focus my energy there, with gratitude. He was coming to America, and we were going to be together again. This is the part where I always get that damn Partridge Family song stuck in my head, "Together We're Better." You're welcome.

Being Myself at Work on Day One

When I started at Ernst & Young in 2005, I'd been back from the UK for less than a month. I'd been over there for a good chunk of my career, so my most recent experiences with workplaces were based on UK workplaces. And I had this weird accent, especially for a guy who had grown up in Southeast Texas and hadn't lived in any other state before the big move to the UK. It hovered somewhere over the open waters of the Atlantic—not quite fully American, though certainly not English. And I swear to God it wasn't put on. It's hard to explain if you haven't lived somewhere else for a good length of time, but it insidiously works its way into your cerebrum, redirecting neurons into new neural pathways that make you say, "I shouldn't wonder" rather than, "I bet." And it's not just phrases. The accent and intonation maintain their roots while picking up fragments of the host. Questions go down at the end, not up. "Can I get" becomes "May I have." And so on. The point is that the way you talk changes. Some people think it's pretentious, while others think it's cool. And even though all these years later, I now sound exactly like you'd expect a Texan to sound, and even more so after a couple of martinis, at that time, my feet, mouth, and tongue were firmly planted in two countries.

Given that I'd been at EY a few months when the visa nail-biter took place, I'd already established myself as gay. For the first time in my career in the United States, my home country where I'd started working as that frightened, closeted twentysomething, I was openly gay from the first day on the job. I didn't have to hide it. That doesn't mean that everyone knew I was gay. Existing as an out individual and making sure everyone knows you're out aren't quite the same thing. At this point, we'd just wrapped up the busy season. In the Big 4, that's the tax filing period for individuals and corporations. We worked long hours from January through April, and as a result, socializing was more restricted than the rest of the year, so most people had limited information about me. They knew I'd just returned from living in the UK. Some knew I was gay based on conversations about Simon. Not everyone got the memo though. Quite a few single females in my group stopped by my little cubicle that first week to chat. They loved my accent. I sounded so sophisticated, worldly. The group was mainly female, so I didn't clock it at first. They were just being friendly. Just popping by to confirm the rumors of my urbanity.

On Friday afternoon, at the end of my first week, my peer buddy Neepa stopped by to see how things were going. I'd liked her immediately when she'd met me in the lobby that first morning. She was friendly, interested, kind, and, most of all, curious. My suit and tie didn't look like they came from around here—did I get my clothes in the UK? Which part of town was I living in? Why would I move back to Dallas after living in London?! I didn't mind. After spending years with the largely reserved Brits who didn't dare ask such seemingly personal questions, it was refreshing to be back among my own kind. But there was one question she hadn't asked.

I was giving her highlights of how the week had gone when she gave me a look that is as clear to me now as it was that Friday. Sheepish (rare for Neepa) combined with a hint of conspiracy. All the girls (her word, not mine) had been talking about me. I must have overheard them talking (I hadn't). They all wondered if I was single but figured I had a girlfriend. But maybe not since I had just moved back? Had I broken up with someone back there and that was the reason I'd returned home? Was that the reason, Jones? (She liked calling me Jones even in that first week. She still does.)

I hesitated before answering. I didn't care anymore that I was gay, but damned if I wasn't concerned about breaking all those hearts. No, seriously, that's what I thought. I'd had so many compliments on my accent this week, looks of admiration for how I dressed; I was truly *up my own arse*, as we Brits would say.

So I broke it to her. No, Neepa. I haven't broken up with anyone, and I don't have a girlfriend. I do have a boyfriend, who will be moving over here once his visa is approved. (When you have a boyfriend, you don't have to outright say you're gay. It's a little less dramatic.) Back then it still felt like a bomb was dropping; it just wasn't nuclear in the same way as if I'd said, "Nope, I'm queer, I'm here, and get used to it."

She slammed her hand on the desk and exclaimed, "I *knew* it! They all thought I was full of shit, but I knew! So, let's see pictures of him. What's his name?" And that was that. By Monday at lunchtime, I was officially gay at EY.

Even though I *existed* as an out person, it was my second *act* of coming out at work, that process I mentioned in Chapter 2. Simpler this time, sure, though it reinforces the notion that we never truly stop coming out. It's the case for many of us in the LGBTQ+ community who work in corporate America, where we may repeat some variation of this process each time we meet a new client, supplier, or coworker. The difference this time around was that there was Simon. Other than the whole closeted thing, being gay when you're single isn't that different from being single and straight. What you do and where you go are different, but if there's no other half, there's no other person to refer to regularly. There are more references to the other person, so being out gave me far more opportunities to refer to Simon rather than providing vague narratives about what I did last weekend. No "Cost of Thinking Twice" decision diamonds to drain my battery faster. Whew!

Reflection

If you are not straight . . .

- What have you done in the name of love for your significant other that you wish you hadn't had to do?

- What have you done in the name of love for your significant other that you are most proud of?

If you are straight . . .

- What have you done in the name of love for your significant other that you wish you hadn't had to do?

- What have you done in the name of love for your significant other that you are most proud of?

- Are there times when people in the LGBTQ+ community might have to do more in the name of love for their significant other than straight people do? Why or why not?

5

Being Gay in Uncertain Times

An Abomination

I might have been gay at EY, but I was still choosing my battles outside of work. EY was an oasis of acceptance at a time when it was still illegal to be gay in Texas. By the way, while the US Supreme Court legalized same-sex marriage nationwide in 2015, it is still technically illegal in Texas, since our legislature hasn't voted to take it off the books. Unenforceable, yes, but still there in black and white as of early 2023.

Back to EY. I didn't believe for a moment that meant that the openness to being gay at the organizational level meant that every employee at EY accepted one's sexual orientation. I knew the churches that some of these folks went to were abundantly and unapologetically clear in terms of what the Bible said about homosexuality. It wasn't just a sin, though Christians were supposed to believe the New Testament, even that part that says, "All have sinned and fallen short of the glory of God." In homosexuality's case, many across the South did and still do prefer an application of the Old Testament, where in Leviticus, it's called an *abomination*. This word makes it far worse than any other sin. Never mind that "abomination" was a mistranslation of the Hebrew word *toevah*. Irrelevant that Ezekiel used the same word thirty-nine (*thirty-nine!*) times to describe things like haughtiness and pride. And absolutely beside the point that these texts have been run through the wringer of translations and political agendas over the course of 5,000 years. Our collective gayness boiled down to an abomination in the eyes of many.

No, of course not everyone held this view. Far from it. But they weren't usually out there protesting *for* gays either. On the other side of the pew, there was no shortage of faithful believers protesting *against* the "gay lifestyle." And they were vocal, whether it was the pastor at First Baptist Church Dallas preaching against it on Sunday mornings or the members of Westboro Baptist Church attending funerals of AIDS victims and shouting, "God hates fags." It wasn't good enough for them to have their religious freedom to believe that homosexuality was wrong; they were hell-bent on stopping the juggernaut of changing opinion in the name of a perceived backstage pass to righteousness.

Even now, nearly twenty years later, it feels like little has changed. According to the Williams Institute at the UCLA School of Law in a 2021 report:

> Over half (57.0%) of LGBT employees who experienced discrimination or harassment at work reported that their employer or co-workers did or said something to indicate that the unfair treatment was motivated by religious beliefs. For many, this included being quoted to from the Bible, told to pray that they weren't LGBT, and told that they would "go to hell" or were "an abomination."

Of those employees who experienced discrimination or harassment at some point in their lives, 63.5% of LGBT employees of color said that religion was a motivating factor compared to 49.4% of white LGBT employees.[4]

Full disclosure here: I'm a practicing Christian. I grew up Baptist before converting from Evangelicalism to the lilting liturgy of the Episcopalian church. None of the above surprises me. At all. As people living imperfect lives, it's easier to focus on the imperfection of others. Who wants all that introspection? Far more fun to weigh in on the severity of the sins of others rather than your own. And if you get to do it with a captive audience at work, where no one has the cojones to tell you to stop, even better.

Jesus said something along the lines of, "First take the plank out of your own eye, and then you will see clearly to remove the speck from your brother's eye." But that's just one man's opinion.

While it's not surprising, what troubles me is the unapologetic nature of folks at the office who feel entitled to tell someone else what's wrong with them based on their blinkered interpretation of a handful of gotcha Bible scriptures. I want to say this is unconscious bias; that once the person becomes aware of it, they recognize the harm it does to the recipient. Alas, it's quite conscious. The unconscious, favorable bias lies in the hardwired belief that they're doing the Lord's work,

---

[4] Brad Sears, Christy Mallory, Andrew R. Flores, Kerith J. Conron, "LGBT People's Experiences of Workplace Discrimination and Harassment," Williams Institute at the UCLA School of Law, September 2021,
LGBT People's Experiences of Workplace Discrimination and Harassment - Williams Institute (ucla.edu).

which isn't always easy or comfortable but is necessary. Which in turn necessitates setting aside doing unto others to call out abomination wherever they see it, even—or especially—in the workplace. And they say these things to you about your sexuality out of love, of course.

Adam and Steve

I've had back problems for years, no doubt due to hunching over this little laptop and banging away on the keys for hours on end. Massages help a lot. Not relaxing massages with hot stones and soothing music; I'm talking about those deep tissue numbers where elbows grind down rock-hard knots hiding beneath shoulder blades. Never have I ever responded yes to the question of whether too much pressure is being applied. Inside, I'm writhing in agony, and I don't care—get those damn knots out that are wrapping around my nerves and traveling in locked-and-loaded packs across my upper back and shoulders.

Back then, I went to one of those meh massage places where they all wore polo shirts and khakis and advised me to drink plenty of water afterward. It was fine. The guy who worked on me was great, which meant that he didn't stay there very long. So, no surprise when I got the call that he had left, but they had a great replacement for him. Was I interested in keeping my appointment? I wasn't too thrilled about someone new, but my back was having none of it, so *what the hell*, I thought. *What's the worst that could happen?*

So there I sat in the waiting area. Dim lights, soft Enya-like music playing just under the hypnotically complementary sounds of bubbles while the knots in my back increased exponentially. Then Derek—

funny that I remember his name more than a dozen years later—came in and asked for Kevin. I stood up, and we introduced ourselves. In near whispers, of course.

He made small talk as we walked through the labyrinth of halls leading this way and that, with door after exact-same door leading us ever onward. We finally arrived at the room, where Derek studied my chart and said knowingly that I must work in an office. After mutual agreeing on the level of torture to inflict on my back and shoulders for fifty minutes, he left me alone long enough so I could get ready. When he knocked on the door, I said, "Come in," like it was my office or house. *Yes, Derek, welcome to my little corner of the world I like to call massage room number twenty-eight.*

Anyway, he got to work, and all was mercifully quiet. No talking. Good. Let me bear my torture in peace, and you do what you need to do to stay focused on the evil lurking near my scapula. Then, damn it, he had to start. I don't remember the particulars of the conversation, just that I was annoyed that I had to make small talk through the sound of bubbles. It started benignly enough and continued its bland course until my radar began to beep. Slowly increasing in frequency as I heard him say something about all the chatter around gay marriage. Beep beep. Personally, he couldn't care less about what people do behind closed doors, but why do *they* have to shove it in our faces? "It's not enough that we have to accept them, but now they want special rights too? It's getting way out of hand. The Bible mentions Adam and Eve, not Adam and Steve." Yep, he sure did go there. That old chestnut.

At once, I pushed myself up from the massage table, grasping the sheet around my waist as I spun around to face this homophobe head-on. "I'm gay, Derek, and that is horribly ignorant and offensive. This massage is over. Leave now and make sure your manager is ready for a conversation when I'm dressed." If you could have seen the horrified look on his face. If I could have seen it too, because that's not at all how it played out. I lay there listening to him ramble on about marriage being a sacred thing between a man and a woman. How personally, he couldn't care less what people do, but they don't have the right to be married. He cared a lot about gay marriage for someone who couldn't care less about gays.

There on that table, I listened without saying a single freaking word. Of course, I was a little vulnerable, naked as I was under a sheet. Who could blame me for not speaking up? Get the massage over with, then make a formal complaint to the manager on duty. Except that I didn't. He ran that one-sided conversation into the ground and grew silent again for the rest of my allotted minutes. When he told me the massage was finished, he left the room; I dressed and walked outside the room where he was waiting. I thanked him—yes indeed, thanked him—and walked to the front desk.

"How was my massage?"

"Great, thank you."

"Would you like to leave a tip for Derek?"

"Yes, please."

I held on long enough to make it to the car, fumbling with the door through the tears flooding my eyes. Angry, ashamed tears. My silence back there was a betrayal of Simon. Of everything we had gone through just to get to this country. Of the life we built together. *Why didn't I say something? Why don't I get right back out of this car now and go back there and tell them what had happened? How many other people like me had he pissed off with his rants? How many other people like me could I save if I just went back inside?* I'll never know. I started the car and drove home.

The good that came out of the encounter with that jerk was that I never lost my voice again. Since then, I've not once sat silently when I hear someone talking negatively about the LGBTQ+ community. I don't go looking for arguments like I might have done when I was younger, though neither do I shy away from an uncomfortable discussion where I know my silence is taken as agreement or acquiescence. Feels like the last couple of years, I've been having more uncomfortable discussions. Rights given can be taken away. I'm not going to sit silently any longer as I watch words turn into opinions, which turn into perceived facts, which turn into action, then violence, or legislation, or legal rulings that could, at any moment, take away the rights that Simon and I never take for granted.

Corporations, organizations, and employers can only protect us so much if a branch of our government has other plans. It's playing out now, with a future as uncertain for us as it was back in 2005 when Simon sat across from that interviewer at the US Embassy in London. The difference now is that, I believe, we are all more ready for it, more willing to jump into that arena and fight tooth and nail for what is ours, regardless of what fringe minority groups may try to impose on us.

And I say bring it on.

Reflection

If you are not straight . . .

- What do you believe in terms of a connection between your spirituality and sexual orientation?

- Have your spiritual beliefs about sexual orientation changed over time?

- Has anyone talked about your sexual orientation with you in religious terms? What was that experience like for you?

- Was there a time when you wish you had stood up for yourself and didn't? What do you remember most about that time?

- Was there a time when you did stand up for yourself? What do you remember most about that time?

If you are straight . . .

- What do you believe in terms of a connection between your spirituality and sexual orientation?

- Have your spiritual beliefs about sexual orientation changed over time?

- Have you ever shared your religious beliefs about sexual orientation with a member of the LGBTQ+ community? What was that experience like for you?

- Was there a time when you wish you had stood up for someone who was gay and didn't? What do you remember most about that time?

- Was there a time when you stood up for someone who was gay? What do you remember most about that time?

6

Just Say Gay

CareerWatch

Promotions in the Big 4 accounting firms are a big deal. They used to be even bigger, back when there was only one promotion cycle per year. If you weren't promoted on October 1, better luck next year. If you were, announcements went out, parties were held in local offices, and you got to change your rank on your auto signature. This was before LinkedIn and the #blessed type of humble bragging you might see now to announce one's promotion, but if we'd had it back then, those humble posts would have been part of the big deal.

From a process perspective, its fixed nature also meant that, in addition to your billing rate going up, certain benefits and opportunities became available to you in that magical month of your promotion.

One such opportunity that opened up for me in that first magical fall of 2006, when I was promoted from Staff to Senior (capitalization intentional), was CareerWatch. It was an EY program in which the firm differentially invested in you if you were a new high-potential senior. But not just any hi-po—a special one. *A minority* hi-po. As a white male, there was only one minority class for me, and I knew it. And after years of subtly missing out on promotion opportunities because of being told I "just wasn't there yet," or "the time isn't right this year," you bet that when the internal link showed up in my inbox, I clicked on it and signed up. Put me in coach, I'm ready to be gay.

Bob was an old-school partner in the firm. In his world, once you made partner, you'd arrived and earned the right to coast. To be fair, I had heard there was an element of historical truth to this paternalistic viewpoint, but the notion had long since gone extinct by the time I arrived at the firm.

In any event, he was never seen around the office on Friday afternoons. The golf course, yes, but the office was a hard no. A partner's desk should never have any paper on it. This rule was about appearances, not tidiness: a partner creates and manages top-dog relationships. They don't *work* on anything—they *review* work that other people bring to them deferentially. Between Monday and Thursday, those other people bring their printed-out Excel worksheets and PowerPoints into a partner's corner office for review and leave with markups. Hard work was always rewarded if you were a white male—bonus points if you came from the same fraternity. That he was sexist or racist, though maybe he was, wasn't the point. It was that he didn't believe in *overt* special treatment. If you were a Black partner and wanted to help another Black person succeed and advance in the firm, that was fine by him. Same with being a woman. But that was a personal decision, not one that the firm dictated to him.

I didn't know Bob well. He didn't pay much attention to anyone who wasn't at least a manager. If we passed each other in the hall, he was friendly enough to greet me by name. But I simply wasn't senior enough for him to invest time or energy into anything more than a basic greeting. Or so I thought.

A few weeks after my promotion, I was sitting in my little cubicle wrapping up a client call—now that I was a Senior instead of a Staff, I had earned, among other perks, the trust of the firm to talk to a client directly without anyone else on the call. I can't tell you how many times I managed to work that into conversations in the months after I was promoted. I had *client calls* in the calendar. "Can we make it after two o'clock? I've got a *client call* at one." "Sure, let's discuss, but I have a hard stop in ten minutes—standing *client call*."

Anyway, I was wrapping up a *client call* when the email blasted into my inbox. *Why on earth was Bob emailing me?* I thought. And that subject line: "Lunch Tomorrow." Not "Lunch Tomorrow?" or "Lunch Soon?" Not a calendar invitation for lunch. It was an email. An empty email with only those two words in the subject line letting me know that we were going to have lunch, tomorrow.

Bob only went to two places for lunch: his business club or the Capital Grille. The business club was his go-to place for other partners or senior clients. Everyone else, he took to the Capital Grille. Dark wood paneling. Booths with green leather. Good tables and bad tables. Judgmental maître d's. Steak and lobster. Baked potatoes. Martinis. Okay, not three martinis at lunch anymore (this was 2006 or thereabouts), but it wasn't out of the ordinary to see all those businessmen in suits and ties nursing a martini over a long lunch, probably fantasizing about their dads' business lunches back in the good old days.

I rode with him to the Capital Grille in his Porsche 911. Thankfully, he spent the entire fifteen-minute drive talking about it. What were we going to talk about over an entire lunch? And good lord, why were we having lunch *at all*? He hadn't said anything when I met him at his office. He was already standing with keys in his hand. "Ready to go," he said. Again, no question marks for him.

Finally, there we were, in one of the good green booths near the front of the restaurant, where you could see everyone coming in. More importantly, they could see you. The menus arrived along with a martini for him. Yep, that kind of place. He'd spoken with the maître d', who told Bob he was keeping his favorite table open for him. That kind of thing still happened. It most certainly still happened at the Capital Grille.

The waiter asked what I'd like to drink. Bob answered for me. "A Tanqueray martini."

The waiter left us with our menus and awkward silence. I was thankful for the menu and studied it carefully. Bob didn't look at his. Of course not. He sipped his martini as I tried to make casual conversation, commenting on every appetizer, side salad, and entrée. I was desperate to fill the silence as I waited for any sign indicating why the hell I was here. Although none appeared, the martini finally did. By that point, I wanted to grab the waiter's arm and ask him to go ahead and bring me two more, but I was interrupted by Bob, who held up his glass toward me and said, "Cheers." I picked up my glass and clinked it against his, quickly gulping down a third of it while he went back to sipping his in silence.

A few minutes passed—two, three, maybe thirty—when he put his martini down and looked at me. "So, Jones, I guess you know why we're here."

Why on earth would I know why we're here? He invited, no, summoned me to lunch. Was I being fired? He didn't need to do that personally. And he wasn't going to buy me lunch and a drink even if he did. I stared at him, drink still in my hand. I couldn't think of a word to say, so I shook my head no.

"Oh, come on, Jones. You know what this is about." He looked genuinely exasperated, like I was playing some sort of sick game with him to make him uncomfortable. He took a big sip of his martini.

Finally finding words, I said, "Bob, I really don't know. I honestly have no idea why you invited me. I mean, you barely speak to me." That last bit was an accident, but the martini was kicking in and my tongue was loosening up.

"God*dammit*, Jones, I'm your watcher. Your CareerWatch*er?!*"

He gave lots of extra emphasis to the "-eer" part as he looked at me. He didn't appear angry. No one in the office was ever in any doubt when he was angry. So what was this? *Think, Kevin, think. The look, it was, what . . . Embarrassment!* I noticed he was looking around the room to see if anyone was looking at us. He had talked to the maître d' with his back to me. As we were walked to our table, not only had he not spoken to me, but he walked as if he were here alone, as if we hadn't arrived together.

I'm not super proud of what I did next, but man, did he have it coming. *Now* I got it: I was a minority, a GAY minority. I had been selected to be in CareerWatch as a way for the firm to differentially invest in my career. And Bob—Bob of all people—was assigned to be my watcher. This was way too delicious an opportunity to pass up, especially now that he'd made such a big deal out of it.

"Why am I in CareerWatch, Bob? I'm not a woman or a person of color. This doesn't make any sense. What am I missing?" Hee-hee. I knew damn well what I was missing, and the answer was "nothing." Now he was embarrassed *and* mad. I could tell he strongly suspected I knew, and I knew *he* knew for sure, so who was going to flinch first?

I don't remember the exact words he said next, but lord, do I remember his face turning red as he fumbled over the word "gay." He just kept rambling on and on about how the firm is differentially investing in me as a high-performing minority. I dodged and parried back with retorts about being a white male. "So what kind of minority am I? I'm SO confused," I smirked.

"Are you fucking playing with me, Jones?" he asked, pissed, exasperated, and embarrassed. "Don't make me fucking say it."

I looked him dead in the eye and said, "Say it, Bob."

Well I'll be damned if the heavens didn't finally open, and this poor straight, white, nice but hot-tempered middle-aged partner said the words: "It's because you're gay, okay?!"

Well, okay then. Now that wasn't so hard really, was it, Bob?

In that moment, over a couple of nearly empty martini glasses, in a noisy chichi restaurant in the heart of Dallas, this man said that three-letter word that, in the past, I suspect he hadn't said as a compliment, if he had used it at all.

I thanked him for saying it and admitted I knew. And then I gave him a piece of my mind. I told him that if he was going to be my CareerWatcher, he'd better get comfortable saying the gay words out loud. That I'm not going to excuse him or forgive him for his discomfort. Not going to make him feel better about whatever hangups he's working on—that's entirely on him. And when we meet up and go through this program, I expect full support. I expect him to go to bat for me when it's needed. And I expect him to say the goddamn words. Yes, Southern Baptist me took the Lord's name in vain. I met Bob on his home turf and scored a victory. He blinked first. Then we both ordered another martini.

The Power of Community Building at Work

Back at my first job in the nineties, we had an electronic system for communicating with everyone in the company. Each person had a unique name based on a standard naming convention. You just clicked on an icon on your Macintosh home screen. From there, you just needed to enter that person's unique name. After tabbing a few times, the screen opened up, and you started typing your message. When done, you clicked send, and that person had your message waiting for them the next time they clicked the icon on their Macintosh home screen. We called it *CoCos*, for "Corporate Communications." The name didn't stick, but the concept eventually caught on.

Anyway, I wanted to mention the first CoCos I ever sent. I don't remember how I heard about it, but word of a gay group in the company reached my ears. It didn't have a name as far as I can recall; it was just a gay group of like-minded men who liked men who liked corporate America. No L, B, T, Q, or + of any sort. It wasn't official since being gay was still illegal in Texas then. Probably wouldn't have been great for the corporate image to be sponsoring an illegal gathering.

The organizer of this gay group sat on the same floor, so super-closeted Southern Baptist me popped right on down to his cubicle in front of everyone on the very open-plan floor and asked him about this big ole gay group and how I might join other homosexuals in enjoying our gay lives together. Pause. Rewind. The organizer sat on the same floor, so super-closeted Southern Baptist me decided to send a super-coded, fumbly, furtive CoCos inquiring if he was aware of any social clubs that he might recommend to me, an obvious straight, heterosexual, non-gay, masculine, woman-loving bro-dude.

I wanted to be covert about it, so once most of the people on my floor had gone off to lunch, I rolled up to my Macintosh Performa 5200, turned on the screen, and waited for it to warm up. Prairie-dogging to be sure no one was around, I sat down, rolled my fancy mouse over the CoCos icon, and double-clicked. Funny that this next big moment is one giant fuzzball. Everything up to this point is as clear as the instructions for inserting a 3 ½ floppy disc. Once the screen opened up and I selected the recipient, nothing. Like I said before, I remember the furtive tone but none of the words. I'd give my right arm and a dot matrix printer to have a copy of that electronic note today, but back then, I don't know how I'd have even printed it. Did we have networked printers? Did I have one in my little cubicle all my own? Whatever, I don't remember, and I don't have a copy.

I do remember that he received the message loud and clear. Later that day, on my way back from who knows where, I turned the corner to see, about halfway down that cavernous floor, *him*. Standing at my cubicle, head *above* the cubicle wall. *Waiting* for me to come back! In front of *everyone*. He was talking to Brian, my next-cube neighbor. *What was he saying to him? Gay stuff? Probably telling him that I wanted to know about gay things at the company and had contacted him, a fellow gay person, to ask about these gay things, so he popped right on down to speak to this gay guy and share more gay details in person.* Everyone within earshot was probably pretending to work but was hiding behind those nicely upholstered walls, listening to every gay word this guy said. By now they all knew I was a flaming, lisping, limp-wristed, self-loathing yet nicely dressed homo.

My face burned as I froze on the spot. I'm deaf in one ear—always have been—but my heart was beating so loudly, I think I heard it in the bad one. This was way beyond panic. This was the fight-or-flight moment of my life, and hell yeah, I was going to flee, if by fleeing I mean squatting below the cubicle walls dozens of feet away just when it looked like he was turning around to look in my general direction. What I did was deliberately drop the papers I was carrying so I had to crouch to pick them up. And wouldn't you know it, as they fell, they got all out of order. Took me ages on the floor to get them back in numerical order. Ages.

When I cautiously stood up and peered over the rows of walls toward where he had been waiting for me, he was gone. Bummer. Heart still pounding in my good ear, I strolled down the main aisle until I reached the branch line of my row, double-checking he wasn't just sitting on the floor waiting to trick me. Assured that he wasn't, I padded softly back to my desk and sat down slowly in my swiveling chair to avoid that swooshing sound of the hydraulic seat.

"Hey, Kevin." Brian was standing in my half door. "Thomas [not his real name] was over here just now looking for you. I didn't know you two knew each other. He wanted to respond to your CoCos. He

91

waited a few minutes and said it wasn't important. Just get back to him when you can." (Besides not remembering the contents of the message, I seem to have blocked out the guy's name. I swear to this day I don't remember it. You'd think I might. So let's just call him Thomas.)

Brian was a nice neighbor. He didn't talk loudly on the phone. Didn't clip his nails or bump our shared wall. We talked to each other over the wall a few times a day but never too long. His only problem was that he was a gossip. And now his only problem was a problem. For me.

"I didn't know you two knew each other," he repeated in Southern code for "How do you know that gay guy?"

"Oh Thomas? He's a nice enough guy," I responded as casually as my collection of plaid Abercrombie & Fitch shirts. "He lives in my apartment complex, and I see him at the pool sometimes. Did he say what he wanted?" *Shit, why did I ask that? Brian already told me he said it wasn't important. Now I sounded suspicious.* Besides that, I didn't know where he lived.

"Nah." He shrugged. "He just said to get back to him when you can."

Like hell, I would. That sonofabitch came down to *my* row to ruin *my* life with all his gay tomfoolery, and I was supposed to "get back to him?" Not only had everyone within three rows seen him, but I'm sure Brian saw to it that those who hadn't seen him knew Thomas had come over to see me. *Wonder why he came down to see Kevin?* he would ask people around me. *I heard he's, you know . . . Do you think Kevin is? He does dress awfully nice.*

No, no thank you. I will not get back to him. At least not by popping down to his subsector of our floor. Back then, I had no idea how email worked. Yes, I know CoCos was a primitive type of email, alright?! It didn't occur to me that a copy of my email might be saved somewhere, so down I sat, screw the hydraulics.

Indignantly clicking on the icon, I fired off a CoCos/email to Thomas, expressing righteous fury that he came over *in person* to talk with me about gay stuff. It was not his place to try to out me, which he was most certainly doing, and don't try to convince me otherwise by coming over in person. Everyone—*everyone*—knew he was gay, and he and I had no reason to be talking to each other. It was *my* right to keep my personal life to myself. He had *no* right to make this decision for me. He knew *exactly* what he was doing by making such a huge unilateral decision. Why is it so important to him to out other people? Why can't he just live his life and *leave others alone*? (The italics are mine today. I don't think formatting text came along until much later.) If this was the sort of behavior I could expect from this group, then he could *count me out*. SEND.

Hooray for me. My first rejection of a community that I didn't know how much I desperately needed, now sitting on an early server waiting to be opened by this horrible gay person hell-bent on ruining my life. Angry electronic words spewing from the depths of isolation, driven by self-loathing and fear of innumerable ulterior motives meant to ruin my life.

Eager to hurl more at him, I waited for a response, but it never came. Days passed. No one said anything to me. No eyebrows raised. My life's rituals continued as before, including running into him occasionally in the elevator. He was kind and gracious, making small talk as if he hadn't received that shitty response. His friendliness had morphed into almost pity, perhaps as a recognition of himself or others he knew who are or were like me. Angry. Ashamed. Wary of the very community that might help me wash the fear of homosexuality away. Admittedly I needed something more along the lines of professional help, but rejection of his simple gesture shut down a lifeline to a support network of people like me. People I loathed because they were like me. A couple of them were cute though.

What a dick! That's what you, dear reader, must be thinking, right? Yes, I was in a way. I was also the perfect embodiment of my upbringing, and lashing out at Thomas was my way of protecting that perfectly crafted world I'd spent a quarter century creating. He had no right to tear it down through guilt by association. Ah, such a beautifully wrapped package of self-victimization and narcissism!

I know he wasn't really trying to. I know this *now*. In coaching, we call it "creating space." It's the ability of the coach to empty themselves metaphorically so that the space that's left is in service of the coachee. It's more than presence, listening, and observing. For those forty-five minutes or so that we're together, we're fully immersed in service to and for them. Through his grace and kindness, his gentle acts of continuing to make conversation while risking further angry outbursts, Thomas created space for me.

So much energy expended for someone who came out a few months later. Yet that space, space I believe he intentionally created for me, drew me in, head above the cubicle walls, to his space as I asked out loud and in person about the group for gay men.

***

Wouldn't it be beautiful if all coming-out stories ended with a neatly dressed, freshly out gay man walking off into a rainbow-filled sunset? #notmystory. My story was a far more interesting tale that needed time before it was ready to be told: sort of a US-to-UK-to-US revolving closet door. I like it better that way. At least now—I didn't in real time. Now, with the ink of the last words of the final coming-out chapter long dry, I get it. I get what other people like me had to go through. And I get that I had to go through it and come out on the other side of that rainbow to discover that all-powerful, craftily elusive word that, though a bit overused lately, fits perfectly: empathy. I work hard as a coach to pay it forward now by creating space shaped by empathy, whatever color of the rainbow my coachee may be.

***

My point is this: without this person who appeared at that moment in my tempest-tossed confusion, I wouldn't have come out when I did. The courage to have that bold conversation with Jeff was forged from the panic, fear, and anger that boiled over on the 14th floor of that massive open-plan office that was way ahead of its time. The suppression of this courage and the renewed sense of isolation that came with it when I went back into the closet nurtured a desire to go back to the way things were—when it felt good to be out, when I had people, a network, communities, who cared about me. Whose flaws were numerous, but homosexuality wasn't one of them. It drove me to come out again, for good. It drove home the almost visceral need for community.

When I returned to the US after my back-in/back-out of the closet stint in the UK, I was out for good. There was the beautiful relationship with Simon, who I eventually married. There were friends across the spectrum, old, new, and in-between, who liked me for the authentic person I'd at last come to love. And there was work at Ernst & Young (EY), where no one cared one way or the other, and if they did, they didn't show it. Fine with me. And there at EY was bEYond (get it?)—a professional and social community supporting all the letters.

My first week there, I emailed the sponsor of the Dallas group to find out how to get involved.

Being Seen with Simon

To come out, you have to say the word. "I'm gay." "I'm a lesbian." "I'm bisexual." "I'm transgendered." And so on. It's kind of hard to come out without saying the password. When you do it, people are surprised, or they aren't. They're judgmental, or they aren't. Whatever the reaction, it's based on the new information you just shared. Once that information is out there, you're just living your life. Not that it's automatically easier after the big announcement, and we likely face multiple coming-out scenarios in our lifetime. But once a particular group or set of individuals knows we're out, there are no big surprises about sexuality.

Having said that, the first time Simon met my coworkers here in the US was the first time any coworker *any*where had met *any*one I was romantically involved with. That sounds so cheesy. Like he was my paramour or beau. By this point, he was more than a boyfriend since we had moved back to the States together, lived together, and had spent the last five years of our lives together. He was my partner and future husband, but he was also the first person of any romantic status to meet people in a professional setting, so I want to be clear that we were far along in our relationship before I mustered the courage to incorporate his existence into my professional life.

In North Texas, the March of Dimes walk takes place every April on a Saturday morning. At my company, several teams form, raise money, and walk around White Rock Lake as part of the walk. Our company is one of dozens. It's usually a beautiful time of year in Texas, before the sun sears every living thing to a brown, crunchy crisp. Employees' families are welcome to participate. On a big field at the finish line, there's a band. Each company has its own tent with food and beer, and there's face painting and balloons for the kids. It's a big, wholesome, All-American party for a good cause. Each company has a T-shirt that their employees wear. Once we all start walking, the closed-off road around the lake transforms into a patchwork quilt of corporate logo colors. One massive capitalistic mob of rainbow colors raising money for charity.

My sub-service line (SSL for the cool kids) formed a group a few weeks in advance of the event. Everyone knew about Simon, but no one had met him yet, so Neepa (yes, the same from earlier), who organized our SSL group for the walk, insisted I bring him. Knowing that, for a Brit, socializing and making small talk with absolute strangers is the worst thing he could possibly imagine, I went home confident that bringing it up would elicit pursed lips. I don't remember exactly how it went down, but it was along the lines of, "Hey darling, love of my life, get this. The company is taking part in the March of Dimes walk, and you're invited as my significant other. How much are you dying to go?"

"That sounded like a marvelously grand idea," he said.

What the hell? Just when you think you know someone. These Brits and their annoying, freakishly spot-on sense of irony.

When Texas in July feels like a high-speed hair dryer blowing in your face, it's nearly impossible to imagine those rare early April mornings when temperatures linger in the forties. On this March of Dimes Saturday, Simon and I threw on sweatshirts over our T-shirts and walked to the park where the event was taking place, lucky enough to live nearby. As we got closer, we noticed the EY tent among dozens of others belonging to large companies that had sponsored the event. Simon shared his amazement at the sheer size of the event, and I replied in agreement. What I didn't say in reply is that I came to this walk ready for a fight, just waiting for someone to look at us even slightly funny—not the people I worked directly with but someone else at the firm, someone I didn't know. It was a big office. *You got a problem with two gay guys walking in the March of Dimes Walk with EY? Huh? Yeah, he's my partner. You got a problem with that?! Part.Ner.* The anticipatory annoyance played out perfectly in my head.

We joined hundreds of others from EY milling about the large tent in the open field at Norbuck Park in East Dallas, our bright Easter-egg-yellow shirts blaring our employer's name and logo. A local band cranked out eighties rock music from a stage (corporate America really does rock you like a hurricane). Kids ran around with their faces painted. We milled about, chatting with people I knew. We ebbed and flowed through various groups, introducing ourselves and meeting others wearing the exact same shirt. "Nice to meet you. I'm Kevin and this is my partner, Simon," I smiled at each new stranger-coworker. "Great to meet you both." They smiled back in reply.

And I mean, what the hell? No one looked at us like we were trying to groom their children. No funny looks, no frowns. Not even the tiniest change in facial expression. Just friendliness and some follow-up small talk. Was it because he was English? I bet that was it. He charmed them with his accent, so he could have been Jack the Ripper and all they'd say is how they loved that time they went to London. I knew, really, that it wasn't that. It was that no one cared. Or maybe they did, and I couldn't tell. Either way, it didn't matter because everyone was fun, and nice, and interested in getting to know us better. My first wonderful macro-experience with the EY bubble.

Still, I can't say I wasn't just a little disappointed. All that practicing in my head last night?—total waste of time.

Reflection

If you are not straight . . .

- What was an awkward conversation you've had with a straight person?

- Do you recall a time when you hid your sexuality at work? How did that feel?

- What are your earliest memories of coming out or being out at work, if applicable?

- If you're in a leadership role, what do you do to make everyone on your team feel included? Respected?

- In what ways might your sexual orientation influence how you lead?

If you are straight . . .

- What was an awkward conversation you've had with someone who isn't straight?

- What do you recollect about the first gay person you met at work?

- When someone identifies as LGBTQ+ at work, what do you notice about your reaction?

- If you're in a leadership role, how do you make everyone on your team feel included? Respected?

- In what ways might your sexual orientation influence how you lead?

7

The Gay Glass Ceiling

Don't Bang Your Head on the Glass Ceiling (Organizational)

With the growth of LGBTQ+ interest groups and organizations creating and enforcing nondiscrimination policies that include sexual orientation, it seems like we'd be seeing a C-suite that's more representative of the organization as a whole, including gay people. Hardly. Get this: According to a 2022 report by Gallup, 7.1% of US adults now identify as LGBTQ.[5] (Remember, this is only people who say they are; information may be understated since self-identification requires voluntary disclosure.) In any case, compare that 7.1% to the makeup of the executive suite: of *all* women-held senior VP/C-suite jobs, LGBTQ+ women hold 0.6% of them. By contrast, LGBTQ+ men hold a whopping 2.9% of all senior VP/C-suite jobs held by men.[6] Still a man's world. A straight man's world.

It would be a fool's errand to make every board, executive suite, and C-suite perfectly balanced with all the colors of the visible and

[5] Jeffrey M. Jones, "LGBT Identification in U.S. Ticks Up to 7.1%," Gallup, February 17, 2022, https://news.gallup.com/poll/389792/lgbt-identification-ticks-up.aspx.
[6] Chris Kolmar, "LGBTQ+ Workplace Discrimination Statistics [2022]: Rates and Trends," Zippia, February 21, 2022, https://www.zippia.com/advice/lgbt-workplace-discrimination-statistics/.

nonvisible rainbow, let alone rebalance it periodically with fresh data. Such a numbers game completely misses the point of equality of access. Still, something is fishy when the numbers are *this* lopsided.

It's also worth reinforcing the previous point that, unlike, say, women or people of color (and I get that people can be both), we LGBTQ+ folks must self-identify before we can be counted. Such an exercise usually involves going into some internal, secure portal on an HR website via a link or survey, voluntarily disclosing this information, and finally allowing the organization to use it. Assume you do all that. What then? Very few organizations differentially invest in career development opportunities for the LGBTQ+ world the same way they do for other minorities. Executive sponsorship for us is extremely rare compared to this type of differential investment in women and people of color. Even at EY, which is extremely progressive when it comes to actively supporting LGBTQ+ causes and equality, the precision of the data concerning women and racially and ethnically diverse members of the 2020 US Partner, Principal, Managing Director, and Director (PPMDD) promotion class provides a glaring contrast to the presentation of this same data for the LGBTQ+ community. While it notes that women make up 38% of the PPMDD class of '20 and 33% are racially and ethnically diverse, there is a single comment on its 2022 Transparency Report that notes:

Our promotees include:

- *LGBT+*

- *Veterans*

- *Persons with disabilities*[7]

---

[7] Ernst & Young, "2022 EY US Transparency Report," 2022 EY US Transparency Report | EY - US

Such data is touted to show ever-increasing diversity among women and people of color who are admitted to and make up the partnership. But did you notice there's not a specific number here, whereas there is for women and people of color? We're grouped into the "Other" category when it comes to the highest ranks of the firm (there is a note about the US population across all ranks when it comes to the LGBTQ+ population: 1.3% for fiscal year 2019 and again for fiscal year 2020). What these groups have in common is that they're self-disclosure categories, so I get that numbers are probably not as accurate as other minority data points. Even so, why not use the numbers you do have and let them stand for themselves? The more you see people like yourself in leadership roles, the more likely you are to believe that this could be you someday. And maybe you're then more likely to self-identify, which gets organizations like EY closer to a true count of their LGBTQ+ employees.

I'm using EY here because I know it well, having been there for nearly eighteen years before I left in early 2023, but to be clear, it's not an EY-specific issue. Companies like Amazon, EY, LinkedIn, Siemens, and so many others who get a perfect 100 score on the HRC Corporate Equality Index struggle with how to capture some sort of representation of us in leadership roles. Nevertheless, it's a bit disingenuous to not differentially invest in our career paths and progressions in the same way as other minorities but then take credit for us being in leadership positions when the annual transparency reports come out.

Whatever work you do, in any organization large or small, it's hard to think of a more accurate or effective means of ensuring faithful LGBTQ+ representation in the upper echelons when self-identification is the norm. And you won't catch me advocating for mandatory disclosure any time soon. But hey, if we lived in a perfect meritocracy (see more on this in Chapter 8), it would take care of itself without the need for differential investment or supporting stats anyway, since 100 percent of the time, the most capable people would have 100 percent equal and equitable access to opportunities and would naturally rise to the top. Since that's not the case, I don't see the point of identifying as a member of the LGBTQ+ community on my official company record when an organization does little about it other than use the data to tout its rainbow-flag street cred.

Back to those lopsided LGBTQ+ numbers from EY—well, no numbers for the PPMDD group and 1.3% of the general population. It's a fair point to say that change like this takes time. Straight women didn't increase their representation in leadership positions overnight. I suspect the increase of Black people was even harder. The difference is one of differential investment in gay careers versus those of women and people of color: in recruiting to get them in the door, in creating an environment of equality of access to opportunities that allowed them to advance, in providing company-blessed mentoring and executive sponsorship that helped address unique issues and hurdles they faced on their way up. When it comes to differential investment in career paths, we're pretty much on our own to figure it out.

The argument goes something like this: "We can't do these things to this degree with people who identify as LGBTQ+ because, unlike women and people of color, the only way we know they're LGBTQ+ is if they self-disclose. We can't force them to self-disclose because that's a violation of privacy. And if we only differentially invested in the careers of LGBTQ+ people who were out, that could be seen as discriminatory against those who have chosen not to be out."

That's not to say that organizations don't support our community in other ways—charitable giving to our organizations, creating a safe working environment that encourages us to bring our full selves to work, supporting the creation of Employee Resource Groups (ERGs), and lobbying local and national government on LGBTQ+-related issues. These are all great things that should not be dismissed. But they simply don't rise to the same level of quantitative and qualitative investment as other minority groups who receive more structured and sustained support as they work their way up the career ladder.

Because of this unbalanced investment, I am super impressed by the people who still made it to the top—out, proud, jumping over hurdles like Olympic athletes (some of whom are also gay!). As that gay glass ceiling grew closer with each promotion, they knew they would either hit it or smash that thick slab to bits. I'm not happy about it, mind you. It shouldn't be that hard for us. Or at the very least, it shouldn't be harder for us than it is for other minorities in whom an organization differentially invests to help them move onward and upward in their careers. Even in most of the organizations that get a perfect score on the Human Rights Campaign's (HRC) Corporate Equality Index, sexual identity doesn't play directly into decisions about who to promote. It might be a lagging factor before finalizing promotions lists along with other DEI criteria, but it's not hard-coded into promotion decisions in the same way as race or gender-based ones.

And why should they? It's not an HRC Corporate Equality Index criteria. And this Index is THE list to be on for organizations seeking to brandish their DEI street cred, and a perfect 100 score is the brass ring for the LGBTQ+ part of an organization's DEI strategy. As of 2022, their criteria consist of four pillars:

- Nondiscrimination policies across business entities;

- Equitable benefits for LGBTQ+ workers and their families;

- Supporting an inclusive culture; and,

- Corporate social responsibility.[8]

Great criteria. Crucial to supporting a welcoming work environment and encouraging organizations to move beyond their own walls to influence their external environments. And this is where things get a little funky for me. As long as this Index remains THE test of your DEI commitment, companies will study for what's going to be on the test. When the answer to the question of "Is sexual identity as a promotion criterion used to assess nondiscrimination policies across business entities?" is no, some organizations may use it anyway, but they don't *have* to get a good score. If supporting an inclusive culture doesn't require sexual identity as a promotion factor for consideration, the same as it is for women and people of color, then most organizations won't use it.

By this point, are you thinking, "Why does this even matter? I get the point about DEI, but where does it end?"

Well, it can end right here. Any organization can say at any time that they've reached their DEI goals and hit the brakes. No one is

---

[8] "Corporate Equality Index 2022: Rating Workplaces on Lesbian, Gay, Bisexual, Transgender and Queer Equality," Human Rights Campaign Foundation, 2022, https://www.hrc.org/resources/corporate-equality-index.

forcing them to go any further. Hell, no one forced them to go as far as they've gone. Strategies, including DEI ones, are deliberately high-level. Any organization can reinterpret its DEI strategy at any time to say they're pleased with the progress they've made so far, there's still more to do, etc., and then do little more after that. But is that what their shareholders want? Their clients? Suppliers? The best and brightest coming out of college who may have multiple job offers?

To be clear, I am amazed by and grateful for the work the HRC has done in this space. Lord knows how far we've come in the twenty years they've been issuing this report. I don't want to think about where we'd be if companies didn't see the value of scoring well based on these platforms. I simply think that because of who they are, they have a responsibility to the LGBTQ+ community to do even more. To score a perfect 100, *organizations should have to include sexual identity as a key input to assessing the diversity of promotion candidates at every level.* And totally fine if an organization doesn't do it. They can check all the other boxes and get a great score, just not a perfect one.

Remember now: 7.1% of US adults identify as LGBTQ, while LGBTQ+ women hold a mere 0.6% of executive-level positions, and men hold 2.9%. This is not a statistically insignificant gap, especially given the low starting percentage of all (self-identified) LGBTQ+ individuals in the workplace. And by the way, requiring a company to *include* sexual identity as *one* promotion factor among many is not the same as *making* a company promote/advance people at the same percentages as their makeup in the general population. It is, however, a simple way to encourage companies to incorporate it into their assessment and decision-making processes.

There are many arguments against this practice, including its impact on people who would still be reluctant to disclose their sexual identity, even if it meant a fairer shot at promotion. Instead of focusing on this possibility, we should be more concerned about the people who are already out who might benefit from including this factor in such decisions. We plant the seeds of a virtuous cycle.

And while doing so wouldn't eliminate the glass ceiling, it might make it a lot thinner and easier to smash.

We Create Our Own Glass Ceilings: Self-Selecting Out of Advancements

In Margaret Atwood's book *The Handmaid's Tale,* and subsequently in the first season of the television series, Offred, the protagonist in the story, discovers a note scratched into the wall of her closet: *Nolite te bastardes carborundorum.* This roughly translates from a literal perspective of Latin into "Don't let the bastards grind you down." As a pedantic Latin nerd, I must say that it's all nonsense; mock-Latin at best. If she really wanted to keep her spirits up through inspirational Latin quotes, she would have scratched something like *nil desperandum,* which means "never despair," and which I believe my high school Latin teacher, Mrs. Emmons, might approve of. Then again, God rest her soul, she made us recite the Pledge of Allegiance every day in Latin.

Anyway, too often at work we let the bastards carborundorum us by creating our own glass ceilings and leaving before we get the chance to climb too far up the ladder, if we even make it that far. Incredibly, as late as 2022, 10% of LGBTQ+ employees left their jobs because the work environment did not accept LGBTQ+ people. And Chris Kolmar's report also notes that one in five LGBTQ+ Americans experienced discrimination based on sexual orientation or gender identity when applying for jobs.[9] In the first case, it's a no-brainer that I'd leave. *Aspirations for career advancement in a place that doesn't even accept me? No, thank you.* In the second case, I suppose I could chase windmills day after day, hoping I'd finally change that culture of discrimination. Probably wouldn't make me any friends and certainly wouldn't create an environment conducive to career growth.

No one talks about that part when discussing the value of meritocracy (see Chapter 8). Our gay careers, and our ability to own and manage our careers as openly gay individuals, are at the mercy of the cultures of the organizations in which we work. A McKinsey study from 2022 noted that coming out is especially challenging for junior employees as well as women:

> Only one-third of LGBTQ+ survey respondents below the level of senior manager reported being out with most of their colleagues. As one person explained, "Being authentic once you've made it is easier than being authentic when you haven't." Yet even among senior leaders, many remain in the closet. Of the LGBTQ+ senior leaders we surveyed, one in five is not broadly out at work. Women are far less likely than men to be out. Only 58 percent of the LGBTQ+ women we surveyed (compared with 80 percent of LGBTQ+ men) said that they are out with most colleagues. One reason: existing

---

[9] Kolmar, "LGBTQ+ Workplace Statistics."

gender discrimination. One interviewee reflected that, as a woman, "you always had to be perfect in terms of how you looked and what you did, and your work always had to be better than everybody else's. So there was almost that thing of, 'Why add anything else to make it more difficult?'"[10]

Imagine those dorm room sorority girls from earlier. They carried that forced-outing experience into adulthood and possibly into their careers. I don't know where they are now, but their story is far from unique. They could be fierce gay-rights champions. Or they're out and living an authentic life. They could be the closeted women who know how hard it is just to be a woman in the workplace, so why create more barriers by revealing their sexual orientation? Maybe they even went back into the closet. Or maybe they were simply experimenting, exploring their sexuality, and college should be an ideal setting for exploring every aspect of who we are. Regardless, a pretty high price to pay, so why should they or anyone else who lived through a similar experience make it any harder for themselves out there in the corporate-America jungle?

Another consideration in this same report is that gay people don't just come out once and are done with it. It's not like you make a big announcement across the organization, to your clients, suppliers, and other internal and external stakeholders. The more likely reality is that coming out is far from a one-and-done deal:

---

[10] Peter Bailinson, William Decherd, Diana Ellsworth, and Maital Guttman, "LGBTQ+ Voices: Learning from Lived Experiences, "McKinsey & Company, June 25, 2020, LGBT workplace discrimination: Learning from lived experiences | McKinsey.

People who are open about being LGBTQ+ often need to come out repeatedly. Nearly half of LGBTQ+ respondents reported having to come out at work at least once a week in the past month. One in five respondents had to come out multiple times a week, and one in ten said they had to come out on a daily basis. One termed this the "multiple coming out conundrum," adding, "I think straight people don't get it." A gay man at a Japanese multinational related: "It's in my bio—I've been out about my family since I joined this company. Still, I have these dinner conversations with senior executives who ask, 'Is your wife Japanese?' It's a constant."

The experience appears widespread: a lesbian partner at an international law firm reflected, "It makes life difficult because you're coming out all the time. We all get those questions from clients, like, 'What does your husband do?'" Having to come out repeatedly can take a toll. One interviewee described the effort in an earlier role as "psychologically draining." Things are better in her current role: "Being someplace where I can just be out, know it's OK, and take that noise out of the system, I do think has helped me focus."[11]

With every new introduction, there's a chance we will find ourselves facing a split-second decision on whether to come out again.

---

[11] Bailinson, "LGBTQ+ Voices."

Kim Cracks the Ceiling (Sexuality Does Not Matter—Performance Does)

Another announcement about upcoming leadership changes came out recently. I like that my firm shares these changes with us; it's useful to know who's going where, when, and why. The communications typically share a bit about their journey to this pivotal point in their careers. These people have worked hard over the years and are committed to the success of the firm while setting an example for others. It's inspiring, even if it is formulaic:

> We are delighted to share with you that CURRENT LEADER will be moving into a new role effective DATE, where HE/SHE will bring deep MARKET/SECTOR/SUBJECT MATTER expertise to grow our evolving business in BUSINESS AREA REGION.

> Taking over from HIM/HER is NEW LEADER, who spent the last X years building out the emerging LATEST TREND practice.

> NEW LEADER has been married to their OPPOSITE SEX SPOUSE NAME for X years and they have Y children together.

As I read this latest one, I didn't feel inspired or informed. I was super annoyed but couldn't put my finger on why, so I moved on with my day.

A couple of days after this announcement, I was working on something for a client, and it suddenly hit me why I had been annoyed.

Even though I'd seen this last paragraph in the template numerous times over the years, this time it hit differently. It wasn't the formula itself but its contents: *every* time these announcements come out, that last paragraph never talks about people like me. Senior leaders are straight, married, with children. I find myself reading these announcements hoping I'll reach a surprise at the end. It doesn't happen.

Actually, I take that back. It happened once, about three years ago, when Kim, a senior partner, took on a leadership role in the firm, and the last paragraph described her life with her wife and three children. I can recite every word of it *because* it was the only one that featured someone like me. I read it and reread it. "Her wife," "together X years." As cookie-cutter, as normal as any of the others. No parenthetical "that means she's gay, everyone." The subject title didn't say "Senior Lesbian Partner Takes on Leadership Role." Just another template with another leadership change. It was the ordinariness itself that made it stand out. Well, it was *also* the ordinariness of it.

And I'm proud that it wasn't about her sexuality; it was just another leadership change that involved someone who happened to be part of the LGBTQ+ community. This felt like the start to normalizing accessibility for all to leadership roles, and I was excited.

And here I sit, writing this, still conflicted. Shouldn't I be happy with this one announcement? It's better than none. My answer is no. One announcement in three years is not the endgame. So, what is? It's not about a quota or a percentage. I can picture that policy now:

> *The firm is pleased to announce that effective with the start of the new fiscal year, for every seven leadership changes announced that involve a straight person, one*

shall involve a gay man or a lesbian (lesbian shall count twice on the DEI scale—one point for being gay and a second for being a woman).

Following on our commitment to the LGBTQ+ community, effective in the fiscal year following, we will add the remaining letters to the formula. We are still in the process of evaluating the appropriate letter-to-points-to-announcements ratio, so watch for more exciting updates as the new year progresses!

Yes, absurd. Of course, that's not the way it should be. But I am certain that it should be more than one. And at least at EY, more announcements like Kim's came over time. I started seeing more leaders who were gay. They headed up ERGs. They posted their own coming out stories internally and on LinkedIn. They were inspirational. And almost without exception, there was a qualifying sentence that went something like " . . . and I'm proud to work for an organization like EY that supports our LGBTQ+ people . . . "

I get it because I was proud too. And grateful that it didn't matter. But woven into that pride and gratitude was a sadness that ours wasn't everyone's experience in the workplace. That much is clear by the "and I'm proud to work for" statements.

Also, as you may be thinking at this point, *why does he feel gratitude? He deserves to be out and himself as much as any straight person.* Oh, amen to that, even if you weren't thinking it. I agree with the sentiment even if the reality of our lives doesn't instill pride in where we work for supporting who we are. Whether it's geographic, socioeconomic, education-based, industry-related, or some other reason, we don't all have the luxury of bringing our full selves to work. As long as this is our collective, if not individual, reality, then I'll be grateful for having had the encouragement and space at work to be my full self.

Which brings me to a related point: People in our community have the option of remaining as invisible as they like. Most of us have made this choice at some point in our lives, unlike other minorities who don't have that luxury. Compared to a person's race, sexual orientation is harder to identify. And unless an assumption is corrected, one is assumed to be straight, which leads to the decision of whether to correct the assumption or remain invisible.

A Black person growing up in a Black family is unlikely to hear racist jokes being told around the dinner table. Young girls might hear sexist comments in their family, though probably not vulgar ones about women. A kid who knows they're gay—or at least knows they're different in a way they can't yet articulate—might hear all sorts of jokes about gay people. As a white male, I didn't experience the same unpleasant past as visible minorities who didn't get a say in what others thought of them. For better or worse, I did have a say. I was aware of negative attitudes toward people like me through jokes, derogatory terms, scripture quotes, and stereotypical gestures, so I had plenty of opportunities to remain invisible to save my self—or my soul.

These memories ride a rainbow wave through time, stubbornly persisting in every aspect of our adult lives, from relationships to careers. Even if we're out now, we know some people still think negatively about us. Those people might do a better job of hiding those thoughts now than their parents did a generation ago and now that they know about us. And with that info, we can still choose to be invisible:

to the boss, neighbor, client, colleague, prospect, or acquaintance. So we correct the assumption. Or we don't.

A company can't ask someone if they're gay; the person must self-disclose, voluntarily. And you can bet that if the company hasn't created an environment where employees feel safe doing that very thing, they won't.

And creating that environment takes time. Work environments evolve in a delicate dance along with societal norms. When I was a kid, I used to visit my mom at her office, and there were ashtrays everywhere—thick glass ones on desks, little black plastic ones in break rooms, and my favorite, the standing pedestal ones where when you pushed a little silver button on the side the two halves of the little bowl split, swallowing up those yummy ashes into the mysterious depths below. People smoked everywhere. Airplanes had those cute flippy-flip lids on the armrests that were teeny-tiny ashtrays. If you're of a certain age, remember knocking on the door of the teachers' lounge at school to fetch a teacher? As it opened, a swirl of tobacco surged up into your nostrils and permeated your clothes. And think of all those matchbooks that advertised restaurants, motels, and plumbing services. And cars? Half the time when my dad flicked his ashes out the driver's side window, they blew back in on me as I sat behind him in the back seat. Society smoked, and that included the workplace.

Then restaurants started having nonsmoking areas. A few more years passed, and those nonsmoking areas encroached on most of the restaurant, leaving the smokers to huddle around a few sad tables near the kitchen. Finally, smoking was abolished altogether in favor of those who enjoyed tasting their food.

The same held true in the workplace. Rules gradually changed until they became norms. You could work for the same company your whole life (not likely these days) and remember the smoking. And the sexism. And the homophobia. Knowing how things *used to be* is a perfectly valid reason for being cautious about coming out, even as the workplace evolves along with society.

As much as workplaces have evolved and societal norms have changed, it's still astonishing to me that it was only in 2014 that the first CEO of a major company came out as gay. Taken from a CNN interview with Tim Cook, the CEO of Apple:

> "I'm very proud of it. Being gay is 'God's greatest gift to me," he said. "I was public because I started to receive stories from kids who read online that I was gay."
>
> He said the emails and letters came from children who said they had been ostracized, bullied or abused because of their sexual orientation.
>
> Cook said he is a private person but ultimately decided that he was being "selfish" by keeping quiet about his identity when he could help people by coming out.
>
> "I needed to do something for them," Cook said. He wanted to demonstrate to gay children that they "can be gay and still go on and do some big jobs in life."
>
> Cook said he was shocked that he was the first out CEO of a Fortune 500 company. He said he is glad other CEOs have come out since, although that wasn't his goal.

Coming out has also helped Cook as a leader, he said.

> "I learned what it was like to be a minority. The feeling of being in a minority gives you a level of empathy for other people who are not in the majority."[12]

Remember the earlier comment that it's easier to be authentic once you've made it? That's not to take a single thing away from Tim's courageous and example-setting act. But think for a minute about that. According to CNN, "His sexual orientation had been widely rumored beforehand though he had not confirmed it publicly."[13] He had made it all the way to the level of CEO *of Apple* before it was general knowledge that he was gay. Imagine if you are straight, having to manage the fact that you're attracted to people of the opposite sex so carefully that you're at the top of the career ladder before anyone knows. Or at least before you confirm it. I think it was harder for Tim to make it to CEO specifically because he had to manage all that secrecy and be the absolute best, most amazingly, perfectly suited person for the CEO position of a company like Apple.

If it took that long at an uber-progressive company like Apple, what would it take where you work?

Setting those companies and Tim aside, how do we differentially invest in LGBTQ+ advancement in the willing organizations if we don't know who those people are? Some question the need at all.

---

[12] David Goldman, "Tim Cook: Being Gay Is God's Greatest Gift to Me," CNN Interview with Christiane Amanpour from October 30, 2014, CNN, October 26, 2018, Tim Cook: Being gay is God's greatest gift to me | CNN Business.

[13] Goldman, "Tim Cook."

First it was women, then people of color. They've made it into the upper ranks and are thriving. We still have work to do, but our investments are paying off. And because many of those women are people of color, and women and people of color can also be LGBTQ+, they've already benefited from these investments, albeit indirectly as an LGBTQ+ person, self-identified or not. As the number of circles and intersections in the Venn diagram increases, so too does the complexity and confusion around decisions on differentially investing in the career advancement of under-represented populations.

Why don't we simplify the whole thing and focus only on high performers regardless of gender, ethnicity, and sexual orientation? You know, be a meritocracy. It worked exactly the way it was supposed to work for Kim. She achieved her success not because of her gender or sexuality but because she was the most qualified person for the role. Why look at any group differently if those groups now have representation in the upper ranks of an organization?

Kim was and is absolutely the most qualified person for the role. On top of that, she's been open about her sexuality and her family throughout her career. Kim was comfortable enough with her sexuality that she allowed it to be a natural part of who she was personally and professionally. And she is setting a beautiful standard for those who follow. The problem is that people like Kim are rarified air, outliers. They succeed despite their sexual orientation or the meritocracy, where people on the inside still tend to be largely white, male, and straight. Meritocracy is a fallacy in and of itself, since merit and ensuing success are determined by who defines it.

In a perfect business world, if you talked about a meritocracy, I'd be straight-up here for it. But we are so not in that world. We're in a world where people don't have equal shots at the same opportunities, much less enjoy the merit that comes out of those opportunities.

When a coworker tells a lesbian that her sexual orientation makes them uncomfortable, it's because that person feels comfortable enough to say that to her. Otherwise, there would be consequences. That work environment is not likely big on the idea of true meritocracy. Ditto for the straight white manager who enjoys working with a straight white junior staff member, so she asks him to work on a future opportunity with her, even though others she didn't consider are just as qualified. Or that VP who sees the high-performing quiet guy who doesn't like to talk about his personal life or go golfing with the group as standoffish and not a team player, so he chooses someone else who will be "a better fit."

Well, so what? What's so wrong with wanting to work with people you like or putting together a team where everyone feels comfortable with each other?

Nothing really. Except now we're back to the whole not-living-in-a-meritocracy world. Now we're talking about differential access to opportunities based on who you know, how you're perceived, or whether the way you interact with others makes *them* comfortable. *Meritocracy and favoritism, however benign, can't coexist.* I suspect that, just like straight women a generation ago, Kim and other out people like her today must work harder than their straight counterparts to gain access to the same opportunities that showcase their abilities and allow them to rise to the top (more on this in Chapter 8).

Mind you, no one's sitting around in performance reviews saying things like, "Well, Kevin's a top performer, but you know, he's *married to a man*." And certainly no one said this at EY, where I was fortunate to have been given equal access to opportunities based solely (at least I think so) on my capabilities and performance. Yet as a coach for people outside my firm, I know firsthand that variations on these types of conversations happen a lot.

Discrimination Thickens the Gay Glass Ceiling

A few months ago, I was coaching Jonathan (not his real name), who was struggling after his supervisor told him that his rainbow lapel pin made the client uncomfortable. Jonathan was horrified. Not because of what his supervisor said, but because he thought he knew the client better and, at the very least, thought this client would address any concerns directly with him first. Easy enough to remove it, but he knew this was about more than a damn pin. Who does a rainbow make uncomfortable?! It's just sitting there, pinned to some bit of fabric. The client had told his supervisor that he didn't have a problem with gays, but he didn't like them "shoving it in his face" by making sexuality a political issue. Now, Jonathan hadn't said a word to the client about his sexuality, political leanings, or personal life. He'd worn a pin on his shirt that was visible on Zoom calls.

His supervisor hadn't asked him to take off his pin. He'd simply informed him that the client wasn't crazy about him wearing it. Not a major spoiler alert to say that Jonathan felt if he didn't remove the pin, there'd be some sort of blowback. Maybe the client would ask for someone new to replace him on the account. Or it would come up later in performance reviews that he's had challenges getting along with clients. Regardless of whether the consequences materialized, Jonathan was working in a place where the possibility existed based on the environment around him. Where the *implication* was clear enough that the choice he was expected to make was equally clear. Right? How can you expect to be seen as providing great client service if your client is uncomfortable with you? How on earth could you possibly expect your employer to have your back with a client who's uncomfortable because of a rainbow-flag lapel pin?

Of course, Jonathan should have expected his employer to support him. But this is where reality bites. No one tied his sexual orientation to his performance. Not directly anyway. *But we have clients we have to support, you know? And all they're asking is for you to keep your gay politics out of the professional relationship. No, no, this has nothing to do with your performance (unless you keep wearing that pin and disrespect your client). Of course, your job isn't at stake (but your opportunities for advancement are probably limited now).* These subtleties of professional reality make it impossible to fight against a system where there are no easily identifiable bad guys with sinister motives, only not-so-great ones with imaginary spines.

Anyway, as a coach, it's a baseline expectation that I don't insert myself into my clients' stories. That is, I follow where they go. I don't try to lead them in a particular direction or tell them what they should do or what I would do if I were them. I listen, ask questions, make powerful observations, but I never get involved in their story. But I really wanted to get into this one! I wanted to tell Jonathan to tell that client he'd be more than happy to take that pin off and shove it up his ass. Or tell his supervisor that he would wear the pin but would *not* work with this homophobic client anymore and dare him to make it about performance. Better yet, ask his supervisor to defend him and his rainbow pin to the client. To. Speak. Up! I know, crazy talk, right?

Instead, I did all the things I mentioned throughout our coaching relationship. I asked Jonathan about the cost of not taking action. I mentioned to him that his energy level seemed lower since that pin conversation. He decided to look for a new job with a different employer, so we discussed his action plan, what he needed to do to move forward with it, and what resources he'd need along the way. He found that new job. It was the right decision for him, and I was happy for him. But I was also angry that there are places like this where people feel their only real option is to not be themselves or leave. Where if they stand up for themselves, they're seen as difficult, not team players, people who *just aren't a good fit*.

Organizations like this often just don't get it. They're simply communicating a client's thoughts and expectations. Why would someone be so sensitive when they're supposed to be there to serve the client? They didn't ask him to lie about his homosexuality. They didn't make any requests to take off the pin. And it's just a pin, right? The organization's first obligation is to their clients, and if a client's uncomfortable, it's the organization's obligation to address it with the employee. *Geez, if he's going to make an issue out of something so small, what else is he going to cause trouble about?* The subtle labels about people like this emerge: they're not good with clients, everything's an issue, they're too focused on a cause and not enough on their work. Once those labels start to stick, you're not going anywhere but out the door.

So they leave. Or they stay where they are and make all sorts of decisions that straight people don't have to make. Jonathan could have taken off that pin and continued with the client. He might have gotten great performance reviews and even kept moving up in the organization. Except for the nagging feeling that if the organization wasn't going to support his decision to wear a rainbow pin, what other types of support might not be available to him as a gay person who wanted to continue to advance his career there? It's why gay people self-select out of the career ladder. Why they choose principles over conformity. Or conformity over principles and the associated compromises wholly unfamiliar to straight people.

It's why the gay glass ceiling is thicker than other glass ceilings.

It's why so few people like Kim make it that far in the first place.

Reflection

If you are not straight . . .

- And you're in a leadership role, do you believe you had to overcome obstacles that weren't in the way of a straight person? If so, what were they?

- What advice would you give to a gay person just starting their career?

- Have you changed employers because of your sexual orientation? If so, why?

- Do you believe your sexual orientation has ever influenced perceptions of your performance? If so, how?

- Have you ever received feedback at work about your sexual orientation? If so, what was it and how did you react?

If you are straight . . .

- And you're in a leadership role, what differences might there be between your journey to leadership and that of a gay person?

- What advice would you give to a gay person just starting their career?

- Do you know anyone who has changed employers because of their sexual orientation? If so, what did they tell you about the experience? How did you react?

- Do you know anyone who has ever received feedback at work about their sexual orientation? What did you say when they told you?

- Do you believe someone's sexual orientation has ever influenced your professional assessment of them?

8

The Ethical Organization

The Social Evolution of the Organization

"I support inclusion and diversity." Whether it's on your LinkedIn profile, a tagline in your auto signature, or a rainbow-themed background you add to your profile picture every June during Pride Month, it's so easy. It's fine for what it is, but what are we really achieving with these gestures? My inner cynic thinks it's nothing more than the blacked-out image we posted on our Instagram pages to support #blacklivesmatter. It's not that we didn't mean it when we did it. It's that it was an abstract show of support at a moment in time, nothing more than an outward signal, lacking any further action beyond the post. But unlike that IG post, when July rolls around, down come the rainbow backgrounds and taglines. We forget about it until next June.

The optimist in me chooses to back up the question, to reframe it. It's not "What are we really achieving?" but rather, "Remember when these gestures didn't exist at all?" It's tough to let go of the cynic and embrace the optimist. Both have their points. Some people absolutely make these annual gestures just for show, but so what? That we do it at all reflects the evolution of our workplaces, which in turn represents the broader evolution of our society. Those people who do it for show? A decade ago, not only would they not have done it at all, but for the most part, those who did support inclusion and diversity wouldn't have even thought of such outward gestures. They weren't part of our shared understanding of how to communicate these ideas, simply and elegantly, through evolving technology. It's a small gesture that represents a big social shift. Baby steps on the journey to something better.

Wrapped within this social shift are evolving viewpoints that collectively drive how people view their workplaces and how they make decisions about the places where they want to work. It doesn't only matter to the lesbian prelaw student that she sees a rainbow background on her recruiter's email signature. It matters to her friends and family that where she wants to work allows and encourages such symbols, hopefully because the values they represent run deeper than an auto signature or a single month in the year. It matters to her school that they are sending *all* their students out into the world where they can be their authentic selves, thrive, and use their education to better themselves and their world.

Again, a "so what" comes to mind. So what if the best organizations out there use these symbols, these gestures, as a recruitment tool? As long as they mirror their more deeply held collective values, who cares? They want the best candidates. And if they don't want the best candidates because of their sexual orientation, they're going to lose out to organizations where these people *do* want to work. Just as great companies develop reputations as great places to work for all sorts of reasons, including how welcome they make all people feel, crappy companies will have mediocre employees providing mediocre products and services, eventually fading out of existence because their myopic views make them mediocre places to work.

For the companies looking to hire the best candidates regardless of sexuality, we don't have to look any further than Pride Month to see how organizations have evolved. Born out of the Stonewall uprisings in 1969, the first Gay Pride parades were held in 1970 in New York, Los Angeles, and Chicago. Growing from there to major and not-so-major cities. Think Pulaski, Tennessee, where *USA Today* dubbed the supporters "Rednecks for Rainbows." A stereotype, sure, but the fact that towns like this in 2023 show their support for the LGBTQ+ community proves that society is evolving, even when it feels like two steps forward and one step back.

Companies are evolving along with them. Unlike those marches in 1970, corporate America literally or figuratively marches in those parades today in a big way. From Lego's "Everyone is Awesome" in rainbow colors to Skittles' Pride packs and Mattel's UNO Play with Pride edition, product branding and placement with creative displays of the rainbow colors is big business. If you're a beer brand, making sure your product is in plentiful supply at the parades and satellite events is *de rigueur*. Even better if you're a main corporate sponsor.

I get it; they're in it for the money. Again, who cares? They're not nonprofits. If they can make an extra buck hawking rainbow-colored Mickey Mouse ears, it's no skin off my, umm, nose. But they ought to be living the values represented by those rainbow branded products throughout the entire year. Organizations that engage in rainbow-washing are rightfully outed when those values are out of whack. Take CVS, which received a perfect score from HRC. According to an online article from Popular Information:

> The HRC statement signed by CVS Health and other corporations said the companies were "deeply concerned by the bills being introduced in statehouses

across the country that single out LGBTQ individual—many specifically targeting transgender youth—for exclusion or differential treatment." On its corporate website, CVS Health says that it is "proud of our long-standing commitment to eliminating discrimination in health care and health care coverage, including our commitment to support the lesbian, gay, bisexual, and transgender communities."

But, through its corporate PAC, CVS Health has recently supported the sponsors of anti-trans legislation in Texas, North Carolina, and Tennessee, including legislation that would criminalize providing gender-affirming medical care to adults and children.

In Texas, for example, CVS Health backed co-sponsors of SB1646, a bill that would "change the state's child abuse law" to make it a crime for parents to allow their children to receive gender-affirming medical care. Under the bill, parents that allow their children to receive gender-affirming care could be subject to "the possible removal of the child from their home." Doctors who provide such care could be "accused of child abuse, which would trigger a license investigation by the Texas Medical Board."[14]

---

[14] Judd Legum and Tesnim Zekeria, "These 25 Rainbow Flag-Waving Corporations Donated More than $10 Million to Anti-Gay Politicians in the Last Two Years," Popular Information, June 14, 2021, These 25 rainbow flag-waving corporations donated more than $10 million to anti-gay politicians in the last two years.

Contrast that with companies who put their money where their mouths (and hair) are:

> Procter & Gamble worked with GLAAD on the Visibility Project, which aims to increase LGBTQ representation in advertising. A minority of advertisers and agencies are actively recommending that LGBTQ people be included in advertising, Digitas' Lomax said. That's why it's crucial for those in the marketing sphere to think about hiring and promoting people who are part of the community.
>
> "If you're hiring [them], if you're paying the people, if you're bringing them on board to your teams or . . . even using an outside resource if you need to, I think that's what's going to change the game, because then it's going to be done from the heart, and it's going to be real," she said.
>
> Through P&G's own vast portfolio of brands, which include Tide and Charmin, it's been using its own advertising and marketing to reflect common LGBTQ experiences. For example, the company's research found that about 60% of people change their hair when they come out of the closet.
>
> "It's a fascinating insight, but it's based on a bigger human insight that hair is one of the biggest ways that people can present who they are in the world," said Brent Miller, P&G's senior director of global LGBTQ+ equality and inclusion.[15]

---

[15] Arshad Majeed, "The Right Way for Brands to Approach Pride Month (And All Year Round)," *Verve Times*, June 20, 2021, The right way for brands to approach Pride month (and all year round) - Verve times.

I respect the P&Gs of the world because of their courage to do right things like this. At the same time, I appreciate that they do not operate primarily for altruistic reasons. They are here to make a profit. But they can do so while being responsible, respectful corporate citizens who care about all their customers. And all their employees.

Arrival Of Gay Data

That we even have quantitative information at all regarding LGBTQ+ representation in the workplace now would have blown my mind back in the nineties. What an indicator of how far we've come. How far society has come. How much our views on one's sexual identity have evolved. Oh yeah? If so, how come 46% of LGBTQ+ workers report they remain closeted at work, according to Chris Kolmar? Here are a few reasons he cites:

- 38% don't want to be stereotyped;

- 36% don't want to make their coworkers uncomfortable;

- 31% fear they'd lose relationships with their coworkers;

- 27% worry that their coworkers would think they were attracted to them.[16]

So, on top of showing up every day, virtually or in person, to do a job alongside our straight peers, nearly half of us feel like we must do

---

[16] Kolmar, "LGBTQ+ Workplace Statistics."

so while remaining camouflaged. And it appears that we have solid reasons for doing so. Let me elaborate on each reason.

- *Don't want to be stereotyped*

The flannel-wearing lesbian who drives a Subaru. The lispy gay guy who wears base and calls everyone "guuurl." The bisexual who we all know is really gay but is not ready to admit it. The transgendered person who's just confused and wants to make life more complicated for the rest of us. Of those who are closeted at work, well over a third think coworkers will lump them into a two-dimensional category. Well, that's just being a little paranoid, right? As nonvisible minorities, many of us get to hear, or better yet, see those stereotypes acted out firsthand. They're making fun of us. This teasing didn't happen only in a junior high school in the seventies in Southeast Texas. It happened all over this country—rural and urban, left-wing and right, to and from every skin color on the human palette.

And it happened in the eighties, nineties, noughties, and beyond. These children of those times, grown-ups now, don't want to be stereotyped. Those memories of being the victims or watching the victims, knowing what their own fate could be, follow them into the office. Even now, kids are bullied for being gay. Just ask the It Gets Better Project, a "nonprofit organization with a mission to uplift, empower, and connect lesbian, gay, bisexual, transgender, and queer youth around the globe."[17] Those three little words: "It gets better." You're not alone. Stick with it. Your life is going to be amazing.

---

[17] It Gets Better Project, "About Our Global Movement," About – It Gets Better.

According to NBC News:

> In 2010, a rash of LGBTQ teen suicides across the US—including Seth Walsh, 13, and Billy Lucas, 15—inspired the gay advice columnist Dan Savage and his now-husband, Terry Miller, to do something. Together, the pair uploaded a video to YouTube with a simple but profound message: "It gets better."
>
> "If there are 14 and 15 and 16-year olds—13-year olds, 12-year olds—out there watching this video, what I'd love you to take away from it is, it really is that it gets better," Savage said into the camera. During the eight-and-a-half-minute video, published to YouTube on Sept. 21, 2010, Savage and Miller talked about the bullying and rejection they experienced as gay teens, and how life got better for them in the years after high school. Their message went viral, and in the ensuing years gave birth to a nonprofit organization dedicated to spreading it.[18]

How many of us wish we could go back and say those words to our vulnerable, frightened adolescent selves? Those selves who grew up not entrusting their dirty little secret to those around them? Who entered adulthood certain that if someone found out, they'd make fun of them, not like them, because they were different? You think I was

---

[18] Julie Compton, "It Gets Better: How a Viral Video Fueled a Movement for LGBTQ Youth," NBC News, "September 21, 2020, 'It Gets Better': How a viral video fueled a movement for LGBTQ youth (nbcnews.com).

dodging and ducking that guy from the gay tech group back in the nineties for shits and giggles?

- *Don't want to make their coworkers uncomfortable*

Imagine carrying the weight of *this* responsibility around. We don't want awareness of our sexuality to cause discomfort to others. Better for us to keep it to ourselves and deal with the little inconveniences of selectively talking about what we did over the weekend. Of course, the lesbian in Marketing doesn't *know* she'd made these particular people uncomfortable. But she sure knows from experience that she made someone uncomfortable. It happened before to many of us, and if it happened before, it could happen again. The memory's lingering sting is stronger than the awareness that this new information about us is for that person to deal with, not us.

Just think about that. Based on actual past experiences, we have had to assume the burden of not making others uncomfortable based on something that has absolutely nothing to do with them. Karen from Finance doesn't like the picture of you and your wife that's sitting on your desk? Well, Karen, I don't like the picture of you and your husband. Your wedding dress is heinous, and your husband's neck is bulging out all over that clearly rented tux. Talk about making someone uncomfortable. But that would be bitchy. And unkind. And *none of my business*. I can feel uncomfortable all I want, but that's on me. If your sexual orientation makes someone uncomfortable, let that sit with them. And let them figure out how to deal with it.

- *Fear they'd lose relationships with their coworkers*

Sounds like some fine, upstanding people to be friends with in the first place. Yet, the past rears its ugly head again. We wouldn't be afraid of this theoretical loss if we hadn't experienced it already. In the mid-2000s, I reconnected via email with an old college friend. The subject came around to our families. She had a husband and two kids, couldn't believe how fast they were growing up, was I married? I emailed her back with the story of how I met Simon and how long we'd been together woven in among other updates on life since Baylor. Now, I'm not naïve enough to think when I hit send that this news might not land well. But we'd been such good friends, I did hope it wouldn't matter *enough* to affect a reconnection after all these years. Her email back got straight to the point. She disagreed with my "lifestyle." The Bible was clear on this point. She still loved me and wanted to reconnect but needed to make sure I knew how she felt. Haven't heard from her since.

While this person couldn't have been clearer about her reasons, losing relationships due to our sexuality takes on subtler forms. I coached a guy who identified as gay. At the time our coaching relationship began, Scott (not his real name) had already come out to his various groups: family, friends, and coworkers. He'd come out a little later, sometime in his early forties. He was single, had no kids, and most people had long ago stopped asking him about his dating life. By the time he came out, when he met the man he wanted to spend the rest of his life with and didn't want to hide this side of his life anymore, as he related it to me, it wasn't a surprise to most people, and most of them didn't care.

Scott worked in a distribution center on the warehouse floor. In this company, everyone on a particular team—machine operators, packaging crew, quality control, and so on—stopped for lunch at the same time. I don't recall the exact time, but let's say his team stopped for lunch at noon every day. As long as he'd been part of this company, that's what they did. This crew of half a dozen or so men brought their lunches and ate together at one of the tables in the break room. Pretty standard stuff. Not long after sharing the news of his boyfriend with his coworkers, who, according to him, seemed indifferent to this latest information, Scott went to the break room around noon. A couple of the guys were there, so he sat down and had lunch, not giving much thought to where the others were. The next day, he found himself alone in the break room at lunch. And the day after that, and the next day. He suspected the reason, though he didn't know where they were instead of the break room.

Come to find out, they'd started eating their lunch outside the warehouse. It just sort of happened naturally, according to one of his coworkers. One of them smoked, and another one joined the smoker outside with his lunch. The next day was nice too, so others went out there with their lunches. It wasn't planned. It just, you know, happened. They didn't invite Scott to join them outside once he found out about their new lunch venue. And they were all still friendly with him: they made conversation during their shifts, said hello in the mornings, still treated him like one of the crew. *They simply didn't want to spend their downtime with him.* He couldn't prove any of this, and he didn't want to make a stink either, so he ate lunch alone.

These microaggressions are called that for a reason. They're tiny, barely noticeable at a macro level. Scott even thought maybe at first he was being a little paranoid, a little too sensitive. Maybe it *had* all started with congregating outside with the guy who smoked, which turned into an informal new place to have lunch. Really? (eye roll)

Though as a coach I'm not supposed to get involved in my client's story or get ahead of him, this was a tough one. I was careful about asking questions that might have betrayed my doubts about his coworkers' reasons. After peeling away the "maybes," I finally thought we were at a point where it was fair to ask: "What is your gut telling you happened?" Then it all came tumbling out. They changed once he came out. They were still nice to him but were deliberately avoiding him at lunch. It's not the same as *excluding,* but they were no longer *including* him. They simply hadn't told him about their new arrangement, a timing which coincided with his coming out to them. Eventually, as part of our coaching work together, Scott made the decision to leave for a new company. Loneliness is a powerful motivator.

That's different, you're thinking. *The first case was an old friend, not a coworker. He can't prove the second one was because the guy came out to his team.* Maybe statistically it's unlikely that we'd lose relationships with people because of our sexuality, or at least less likely now than once upon a time. Maybe it's irrational. But yeah, it also still happens. As in this case, it's simply more subtle nowadays.

- *Worry that their coworkers would think they were attracted to them*

Wait, what? Seriously? *You? Look at yourself—I can do way better than you, my straight acquaintance.* Of all the reasons given, this one is at once both laughable and saddening.

Alex, a guy I coached, was in his midthirties. He was a few years into his first team-leadership role. One of the most genuinely positive people I've ever met, he was an encouraging, motivating leader who took the time to get to know his team members and help them progress in their careers. Not just a select few—all of them. That he was gay in a large organization, where everyone was encouraged to bring their full selves to work, wasn't part of our work together specifically, it was more just another fact about a person that helps me understand them better in a coaching relationship.

Not only was being one's authentic self encouraged, but I also sensed from our conversations that at all levels of the organization, the culture was built on this sort of transparency and respect. At an organizational level, Alex felt supported. Then he told me about an experience with a straight member of his team that happened in the restroom. He and this straight male got along well—they made small talk in the office kitchen and worked well together on the team. The team member was a solid performer who respected diverse opinions and was eager to continue learning and growing in his career.

The team often went to lunch together. On one of these lunch occasions, Alex and this guy ran into each other as they both headed to the restroom before lunch. Alex said hello to him as they both walked in. Seeing that one of the three urinals was occupied, Alex walked up to an unoccupied one and started doing his business. The other guy bent down to tie his shoe, which seemed to Alex to take a while. Then the guy blew his nose, checked his hair, and answered his phone that wasn't actually ringing, rushing out of the restroom to "take his call." As soon as Alex walked out, the guy's call immediately wrapped up, and he went into the restroom, telling Alex he'd just be a minute.

Curious, I asked Alex what his gut told him was going on. His face flushed as his voice took on a more forceful tone. His gut told him that this was a straight guy he thought he knew, who thinks homos want to get in his pants. Or at the very least, wants to stand next to him and watch him pee for some weird reason.

Talk about a stereotype, and I mean one that many of us gays have about a certain type of straight man! I don't have a clue how rare or prevalent this type of thinking is today. It has never happened to me, at least not that I've noticed. But to Alex, while it should have said a lot about the other guy, and he was visibly angry about the incident, he was more concerned that *he* had done something to make this guy uncomfortable. How could they work together knowing what he knows now about how this guy views him? By going to the bathroom at the same time as him. To pee. Guessing the guy thought that the mere sight of his penis could send Alex into an erotic maelstrom of uncontrollable horniness. Yet it's another way we burden ourselves and make decisions based on the weight of others' biases. We put their concerns above our freedom. There's even a term for it: Covering. According to the same 2021 report from the Williams Institute:

> Many LGBT employees reported engaging in "covering" behaviors in order to avoid harassment or discrimination at work, including changing their physical appearance; changing when, where, or how frequently they used the bathroom; and avoiding talking about their families or social lives at work. Some of the respondents reported engaging in these

covering behaviors because their supervisors or co-workers explicitly told them to do so.[19]

And this is heartbreaking but not at all surprising, from the same report:

> Transgender employees were significantly more likely to engage in covering behaviors than cisgender LGB employees. For example, 36.4% of transgender employees said that they changed their physical appearance and 27.5% said they changed their bathroom use at work compared to 23.3% and 14.9% of cisgender LGB employees.[20]

Aside: While I'm focused mostly on what it's like to be LGBTQ+ in the workplace, it's useful to remember that I'm talking about the people who made it in at all. As late as 2020, a full one-third of LGBTQ Americans reported that discrimination was a moderate or significant factor affecting their ability to be hired, according to an article entitled "The State of the LGBTQ Community in 2020." Income magnifies this impact: that one-third jumps to 47% of the LGBTQ community earning less than $25,000 per year and drops to 26% of those making $100,000 or more per year.[21]

---

[19] Brad Sears, Christy Mallory, Andrew R. Flores, Kerith J. Conron, "LGBT People's Experiences of Workplace Discrimination and Harassment," Williams Institute at the UCLA School of Law, September 2021, LGBT People's Experiences of Workplace Discrimination and Harassment - Williams Institute (ucla.edu).

[20] Sears, "Workplace Discrimination."

[21] Sharita Gruberg, Lindsay Mahowald, and John Halpin, "The State of the LGBTQ Community in 2020: A National Public Opinion Study," Center for American Progress, October 6, 2020, The State of the LGBTQ Community in 2020 - Center for

Imagine, dear straight reader (and dear gay readers, feel free to get uncomfortable about what resonates here for you), having to make a gazillion microdecisions like the ones above every day. Remember those decision diamonds in "The Cost of the Closet" from Chapter 3? Now imagine piling the following additional stressors from the same source on top of that warm, steaming pile of stats:

- *54% of employees who are out at work remain closeted to their clients and customers.*[22] Keeping track of who knows and who doesn't—if you get it, you get it. Remember the lesbian attorney who had to come out repeatedly? How fun is that?

- *26% of closeted individuals wish they could be out.*[23] Wow. A quarter of the gay huddled masses in corporate America are yearning to breathe freely while suffocating under the self-imposed fears of being stereotyped or negatively affecting relationships with their coworkers. Or they work in an environment where being out is a career-limiting path.

- *Around 0.5% of Fortune 500 board directors—of the approximately 5,670 board seats available—were openly LGBTQ+ in 2022.*[24] As one point of reference, and there are many on this subject, Gallup polls suggest that between 5.7% and 7.1% of adults self-identify as LGBTQ+ in the US.[25] So why does this matter? According to Fabrice Houdart of the Board of Outright Action International:

American Progress.

[22] Kolmar, "LGBTQ+ Workplace Statistics."

[23] Kolmar.

[24] Ross Pounds, "Global Diversity Review: New Report Illuminates Global Diversity in the Boardroom," Diligent, September 12, 2022, https://www.diligent.com/insights/.

[25] Jeffery M. Jones, "LGBT Identification in U.S. Ticks Up to 7.1%," Gallop, February 17, 2022, https://news.gallup.com/poll/389792/lgbt-identification-ticks-up.aspx.

There is enormous power in the Fortune 500 boardrooms, and underrepresentation perpetuates the economic marginalization of LGBTQ+ people. Encouraging board members to disclose their sexual orientation and gender identity is a step towards addressing the issue in the conservative corporate governance world. Companies that disclose sexual orientation and gender identity dispel the myth that Directors are unwilling to self-disclose. Interestingly, very few of the Fortune 500 companies that have out LGBTQ+ Board members disclose it in their proxy statements.[26]

Remember that person in the McKinsey study in the last chapter who said, "Being authentic once you've made it is easier than being authentic when you haven't." I couldn't find stats on how many of those same individuals were gay the entire way up their career ladder. If you find anything, let me know.

- *50% of non-LGBTQ+ workers report no openly LGBTQ+ coworkers at their job.*[27] This one is simultaneously poignant and intriguing. Why are there no openly gay coworkers? Do gay people not want to work at those places? Do they work there but aren't out to anyone? Do they work there but aren't out to this 50% ? And if the latter, why don't the gay folks feel comfortable being out to them? Way too

[26] Fabrice Houdart, "Meet the Out LGBTQ+ Corporate Board Members in Fortune 500," Medium, June 7, 2022, https://fhoudart.medium.com.

[27] Kolmar, "LGBTQ+ Workplace Statistics."

much speculation here, I know. But I also know that far too many of us have encountered people like this at work for it to not *somehow* play a part in our decisions about who we come out to.

Remember Keith, that twelve-year-old kid in the first chapter? He learned quickly that not everyone likes the gays. There are still lots of those kids out there, carrying old adolescent fears in their forty-year-old bodies.

- *LGBTQ+ women are more than two times as likely as straight women to feel as though they cannot talk about themselves or their life outside work.*[28] Talk about a double whammy. Not only are you up against all the usual workplace biases against women, regardless of sexuality, but now you're layering on being a *lesbian*? When straight women are still told that they have "sharp elbows," or receive feedback that they're too aggressive in meetings, it's not exactly the kind of environment where you're eager to be seen as being troublesome because you talk about your personal life.

- *LGBTQ+ women who are open about their sexuality at work are half as likely (8%) to plan to leave their current employer in the next year* compared with their closeted peers (16%) and are a third more likely to plan to stay for five years or more (51% versus 38%).[29]

---

[28] Kolmar.

[29] Kolmar.

Well, so what? What if you're not LGBTQ+? What difference does any of this make to you and how you show up at work? Or run your business? Consider this from the academic institution IMD:

> Creating a great place to work is crucial to attract and retain top talent and key skills. 72% of allies say they are more likely to accept a job at a company that is supportive of LGBT+ employees. Moreover, "out" employees in safe environments contribute more to the business than closeted employees in a hostile environment: they are 20% to 30% more productive, trust their employer more, are more satisfied with the rate of promotion, and feel more loyal to the company.[30]

Not only do allies—those who actively support the LGBTQ+ community—care about how their employer supports the community, but out employees clearly care about how their employer supports them, and they show it by giving back more through productivity. And the evidence around LGBTQ+ customers is clear. In a national survey conducted by Harris Interactive way back in 2011,

> [N]early nine out of ten (87%) LGBT adults said they are likely to consider a brand that is known to provide equal workplace benefits for all their employees. 23% of LGBT adults say they have switched products or services because they found a competing company that supports causes that benefit the LGBT community—

[30] Mikolaj Jan Piskorski, Ina Toegel, and Maude Lavanchy, "Thrive as an LGBT+ Executive or Ally," IMD—International Institute for Management Development, October 2022, https://www.imd.org/research-knowledge/articles/thrive-as-an-lgbt-executive-or-ally/.

assuming that other factors like price, quality and convenience were not considerations.[31]

There is a final factor that Kolmar doesn't explicitly call out, since it's not a reason gay people are closeted, though it's often noted by straight people as a source of discomfort: "politicizing" one's sexuality in the workplace. *"Why do people have to talk about their sexuality at all? I don't care who anyone sleeps with, but why do 'they' have to bring it up? I get it, he's gay. Why is he always shoving it in my face? We're already so polarized, why do people have to bring up issues like this at work?"*

What these folks mean is "Why do non-straight people have to bring up non-straight things at work?" They don't see anything political about talking about their weekend plans with their opposite-sex spouse. Likewise with weddings, baby showers, vacations, kids' events, in-law visits, and family illnesses. These are simply everyday or special occasions to be shared and celebrated—there's no ulterior motive, no nefarious intent. Only when it becomes about a member of the LGBTQ+ community does the perception shift. Overlay these same conversations with a non-straight person as the source, and now it's about politics and issues in the workplace, an agenda that "they" are trying to push through. Not all straight people have this bias. Not by a long stretch. Though when the misguided notion of politicization of sexuality does come up, it's a safe bet that it's most likely a straight person who raises it.

---

[31] Harris Interactive, "LGBT Adults Strongly Prefer Brands That Support Causes Important to Them and That Also Offer Equal Workplace Benefits," PR Newswire, July 18, 2011, prnewswire.com/news-releases/lgbt-adults-strongly-prefer-brands, https://www.prnewswire.com/news-releases/lgbt-adults-strongly-prefer-brands.
LGBT Adults Strongly Prefer Brands That Support Causes Important to Them and That Also Offer Equal Workplace Benefits (prnewswire.com)

And as a minor final point, I don't want to think about who *any* of my coworkers sleep with.

Building Organizational Trust (Internally and Externally)

Meritocracy and Privilege

A few months ago, I was scrolling through the Fishbowl app to see what people were saying about the announcement of our new leader, who happens to be female. The outgoing leader was also female. Now, I get that Fishbowl is not an objective source of information or a balanced representation of opinions. What it does do well, though, is provide great insight into what people think about their organization when anonymously sharing their thoughts.

Most of the threads were unsurprising: Why two women in a row? Why two *white* women in a row? Why not a Black person? Why is our world so biased against straight white men? You get the idea.

Then I came across this thread: Why can't we just have a meritocracy? Why does gender, race, or any other factor at all play into it? Haven't we moved beyond these variations on the affirmative action theme? Seems like a benign enough, even sound line of logic: the best person for the job gets it. Talent, effort, and achievement are the only objective factors that should be in play.

Typically, I'm a Fishbowl lurker—I read comments and sometimes like or love or smile at a few. I don't post. Until this one. It's Fishbowl, so I kept it short, but now I get to elaborate on what irritated me about this post.

The very concept of a meritocracy is based on a set of rules and criteria that lay out what merit looks like. Rules and criteria developed and honed over generations by straight white men and biased in their favor. If you fail to notice the bias, you're probably a member of the club because the rules were written for you. Furthermore, the notion of a meritocracy assumes everyone within an organization has equal access to opportunities. This has never been true. If you have ever been given an opportunity to work on a project because of your relationship with the decision-maker, you don't work in a meritocracy. Got the job because your parents know the recruiter who moved your résumé to the top of the electronic stack? You most certainly aren't part of a meritocratic organization.

Is this a terrible thing? The decision-maker gave an opportunity to someone they know will do well on the project. You might have landed the job without your parents' help. That's not the problem. It becomes a problem when the beliefs and actions of an organization are out of alignment. An organization espouses the principles of a meritocracy, but the individuals who make up that organization make decisions about hiring, teaming, upskilling, and other differential opportunities based on less principled factors. Yes, you may believe that a meritocracy is the fairest way to go, but why would you turn down an opportunity to work on a great project just because you know the person in charge? You know the recruiter and you're *not* going to talk to them about your child's résumé? See, none of these things fall into the sinister category. It's those relationships at the individual level that matter more than supporting the principles of meritocracy at the organizational level.

And to be fair, we in the LGBTQ+ community are just as guilty of favoritism as anyone else. I mean, geez, collectively for years, we've been denied opportunities because of our sexuality in subtle and not-so-subtle ways. Why *shouldn't* we make up for those injustices by giving a leg up to people like us whenever we can? I've done it myself using that very rationale. And the people I've done it for performed well. But I recognize that we can't have our cake and eat it too. Either it's right for everyone or it's wrong. It's a meritocracy or it isn't, regardless of the rationalization. But until I see authentic and consistent equality of access in the workplace, hypocritical as that may be, I won't promise not to do it again. Moral relativism at its finest, I know.

Internal Trust and Organizational Values

For me to trust that my company is doing the right thing by gay people, I need to *believe* that these things are important to the organization: actively stamping out discrimination, recruiting at universities that provide a strong LGBTQ+ student support network, and investing in and promoting gay people the same way they do with women and people of color. A company can talk about its importance until they're blue (or any other color of the rainbow flag) in the face. What are they doing about it? How consistently are they doing it? What data and qualitative evidence do they have to back up what they're doing? What views do they hold and articulate out there in the real world that reinforce what they tell us as gay employees? At its core, to be seen as sincere, an organization must consistently *do* what it says it *values*. When I only hear the values espoused and don't see the actions that give those values teeth, I question the company's sincerity. I don't believe they mean what they say. And if I don't believe what my employer says, it follows that I'm not going to trust what they do.

They're happy to *say* the right things when it comes to the LGBTQ+ community, but consistently *doing* the right things is harder. Why is it more difficult to do the right things for gay people when you know what they are? It shouldn't be. That is the bias.

On a final note about internal trust, in the short term I might continue to work at a place where what they say and do aren't aligned, but if my and the company's core values aren't aligned, I'm less likely to stay for the long haul.

Reflection

If you are not straight . . .

- How important is it to you that your employer commemorates Pride Month?

- What are your criteria for determining your employer's commitment to the LGBTQ+ community throughout the year?

- Does the level of support that a business shows to the LGBTQ+ community affect your purchasing decisions? If so, how?

- Do you think a straight coworker has ever been uncomfortable being around you because of your sexual orientation?

- Have you ever been concerned that a straight coworker thought you were attracted to them?

- Do you believe your work environment fosters meritocracy? If so, how?

If you are straight . . .

- What are your thoughts about businesses getting involved in Pride Month?

- Does the level of support that a business shows to the LGBTQ+ community affect your purchasing decisions? If so, how?

- Have you ever felt uncomfortable being around an LGBTQ+ coworker? If so, what was the situation, and what did you do about it?

- Have you ever believed an LGBTQ+ coworker was attracted to you? If so, what reasons did you have for this belief?

- Do you believe your work environment fosters meritocracy? If so, how?

9

Embracing Compassion

Letting Go of Stereotypes

One of my coaching clients, Sarah (not her real name), worked in the financial services industry. She was going through a doldrums phase in her personal and professional life. Nothing was exciting anymore. When she was younger, she wanted to do something—she wasn't sure what professionally—but something where she made a positive impact on the larger world around her. Sarah's first job was working in emerging markets with a large global bank, which was perfect for her personal and career aspirations. As the years passed and she continued to perform well, she took positions of greater responsibility, made more money, moved back to her hometown, got married, had kids, bought a bigger house, made even more money, and sort of lost the plot. Her life was comfortable, but she felt like a sell-out to her younger self. She wanted to work on what the next chapter of her career might look like, which is how we came to know each other.

During one of our coaching sessions, we were discussing her reawakened need for connection. She had poured so much time into work during the pandemic, spending a big chunk of her waking hours working at home.

As we continued to chat, Sarah shared a story. A leadership reshuffle at her company had put her in charge of a new group of people, most of whom she didn't know. Because her new leadership team was spread across the country, she scheduled virtual coffee chats with each of them. No agendas, no specific work talk—just getting to know each other, whatever they felt comfortable sharing. What could possibly go wrong?

As she got to know the team members one by one, she noticed a diversity of interests, backgrounds, and personalities. The conversations were enjoyable—a great opportunity to connect like in the "before times" when she might have invited them out for lunch or coffee. She admitted in hindsight that she probably should have spaced the conversations out a bit more. As it was, she had lined them up back-to-back over a few days to better get into the groove rather than jumping back and forth between these and the usually intense calls related to topics around her new role.

I get the objective. I often conduct stakeholder interviews back-to-back. Gets me in the zone. I get comfortable with the questions I'm asking. The discussion is more free-flowing with the other person. It feels less scripted when the questions come up naturally because I've been asking them over the course of several calls and can pivot more easily based on their responses. It's also a more efficient use of brain energy because I'm not dipping in and out of my talk track with stakeholders, trying to remember for the sake of consistency if I've asked everyone the same core questions. I think that was her well-intentioned goal, though a series of stakeholder interviews where consistency is beneficial is a bit different from an unscripted get-to-know-you chat. So yeah, if you're thinking, *uh-oh*, about now, keep reading.

On this particular day, Sarah was on a roll. She had just wrapped up a call with a guy who was easy to talk to and a great conversationalist. He opened up about himself and what he liked to do in his free time. They both had similar interests, were around the same age, and talked about their spouses and children, who also were around the same ages. They agreed they'd have to meet up when one of them was in the other's town.

She opened the Teams chat for her next call, feeling good about this team and eager to continue learning about the others. When Andy (not his real name) joined on video and said hello, they introduced themselves, and she made a quick scan of what she saw on-screen. Polo shirt, short hair, trimmed beard, somewhere in his late thirties or so, she figured. Sarah unconsciously placed him in her "normal" category, which was reinforced when they began their chat and discovered they'd both attended the same university. She was a few years older than Andy, so even though they hadn't been there at the same time, they shared stories about the same hangouts, some of the same professors, and small world, she had dated a guy from Andy's fraternity. Imagine that. Two middle-aged white people with all these wonderful shared experiences! The fraternity dances, the social activities, the bonds of a shared alma mater where lifelong friendships begin.

They moved on to other topics, Sarah thrilled at these little coincidences. She shared about her personal life—family, kids, hobbies, and so on. During the chat, Andy scratched his nose with his ring finger, upon which there was indeed what appeared to be a wedding band. At the next pause in the now-comfortably flowing conversation, she commented on what she saw. Here I'm paraphrasing a bit, but not much.

"I see you're married as well. Do you and your wife have kids?"

Here was someone new but not. Familiar through shared experiences of place and belonging. A chance to reconnect with a fellow alum as life got back to whatever our post-pandemic normal was turning out to be. Getting to know someone new but not entirely unfamiliar.

As these happy thoughts raced through her mind, Sarah noticed the tiniest change in Andy's facial expression. The energy level had dropped to near zero. She struggled to articulate it other than to say that it was palpable and uncomfortable as the silence stretched out before them.

Then Andy spoke. He said he was married to a man and that they'd been together for X number of years. He went on to talk about how they'd met, what his husband does for a living, and what they like to do in their spare time. To Sarah, it was clear that Andy had been in this situation before and deftly handled it, taking up the question and reframing it to move them on from the awkwardness of Sarah's question. But she barely heard Andy's response. Her face flushed. The sound of her heartbeat thumped against her eardrums. She was sweating nervously.

She was grateful to Andy for pulling her out of his embarrassing faux pas while at the same time incredulous that she had committed it in the first place. Sarah wasn't some backward-ass homophobe, nor was she the type to claim some of her best friends were gay. She truly didn't care about a person's sexual orientation. But, as she explained, she thought she and Andy were alike. In her college world, all the guys dated girls; no one was gay. *Well, not yet anyway.*

Though the conversation recovered somewhat and ended on an upbeat tone, Sarah was horrified at what Andy must be thinking about her now, a stereotype of a homophobic Karen who thinks everyone in her little world is—or should be—just like her.

That's the thing about stereotypes. They don't always show up as nasty, fire-breathing, bigoted dragons, spewing toxic words and actions about people unlike us. They can prey on our comfortably evolved selves as memories of who we were, who others were around us, from a time that no longer exists, reemerging in benign desires to return to a point of our lives that was easy and uncomplicated by the demands placed on our current selves.

In Sarah's case, yes, she stereotyped Andy as a straight guy. Or, rather, Andy didn't fit her stereotype of a gay guy. I mean, geez, there was the ring. He dressed *normally*. He didn't *sound* gay. She was ashamed as she said these words to me. She was thinking it in the moment, even though she could not remember ever thinking this way before. That's the other thing about bias. It takes some sort of trigger for it to manifest as a perceived stereotype. Some information emerges that contradicts our core beliefs. The evidence presented to Sarah reinforced a deeply held bias about how straight men behave compared to gay men. Because he didn't *act* gay, the possibility that he *could be* gay never occurred to her.

That bias by itself isn't good or bad. Everyone has biases, both conscious and unconscious. The moment a bias comes to life in some way is when things get interesting. In this case, Sarah's beliefs about her college days, the way people talk, their gestures, all came to life, out of this person's mouth, as a microaggression that Andy was adept at handling. It was small comfort to Sarah, who was struggling with this new and unsettling information about herself.

We dug into this newness over the next couple of sessions. Together, we uncovered that what bothered her the most wasn't that she had said these embarrassing things, although she was truly horrified when she said them. No, what ate at her was that she hadn't been aware of this bias until the words fell out of her mouth. In Sarah's case, she and her husband *did* have lots of gay friends, who *did* act a certain way, so she thought of herself as an informal expert on playing the gay/not-gay guessing game. Andy didn't act like any of her gay friends, so to her unconscious mind, he wasn't gay.

It was an unconscious bias that hadn't seen the light of day because, in her words, she didn't see herself as an ignorant Karen. Only jerks thought of gay people that way. Or so she believed, until she had her out-of-body experience and saw herself being the asshole.

To be clear, I don't think Sarah's an asshole. She discovered new information about herself that she didn't like and gave it a harsh label. It created discomfort but also eliminated the unconscious aspect of her bias. That awkward moment with Andy provided the key she didn't know she needed to notice how she thinks about people who are different from herself and the assumptions she makes about them. If Sarah hadn't taken that awkward moment and turned it into an opportunity, *then* she would have been an asshole.

And the retelling of this horrifying incident fetched a raucous round of shocked laughter from her gay friends.

Feels like this is a good place for me to make an ugly confession: we in the LGBTQ+ stereotype each other. Remember that 38% who aren't out because they don't want to be stereotyped at work? Who knew that part of that concern stems from the fear of being stereotyped by the very group that works to create a more accepting environment for coming out?

I've done it. I'm not proud of it, but there you go. I knew a married guy at work who had a wife of thirty-plus years and three kids. No evidence to support a view that he was gay. Plenty to contradict it. But I just knew he was gay. *I mean, look at the way he talks, and his hand gestures. And he dresses just a little too nicely for a straight guy, right? And that bitchy sense of humor.*

The other gays and I in the office speculated nonstop about what his situation was. Our collective "gaydar" beeped like crazy whenever he was around. We admired his leadership while also feeling sorry for him that he didn't feel comfortable coming out, even though we all concurred he should. Nice. Supportive. Unconscious bias against the LGBTQ+ community is alive and kicking from within.

An episode of the American sitcom *Modern Family* captures this bias with hilarious accuracy. Cam and Mitch, a gay male couple, were two of the main characters in the ensemble cast. Their young daughter didn't get along with a boy at school, so they went to the school to meet with the principal and the boy's parents. To Cam and Mitch's surprise, the boy's parents were lesbians. While Mitch tried to be friendly with them, Cam and one-half of the couple took an immediate dislike of each other.

As the conversation between the two couples grew more heated, the principal interrupted them to give them an assignment: arrange a play date for the two children so the couples could figure out how the kids could get along better.

"We'll host, obviously," Cam smugly piped up, arms crossed.

"Obviously?" one of the lesbians questioned indignantly.

"Well, I assume you have an unfinished woodworking project at your house."

I'm not gonna lie. My husband and I cracked up. We replayed it several times. We weren't laughing at Cam being mean; we were laughing at how accurate these perceptions were. Uncomfortable as it was to admit, I had similar stereotypes about lesbians. Clearly I wasn't alone, since an entire scene of one of the most popular sitcoms of that period was dedicated to acting out these perceptions. Humor in discomfort.

It worked both ways too. The lesbian retorted, "I look forward to your frittata."

Butch lesbians. Effeminate men. Handy with tools. Handy with a spatula. We all have these biases. In this case, it wasn't even close to being unconscious. Not only were they fully aware of them, but they acted on them publicly while their respective other halves made earnest yet futile attempts to stop them from saying another word.

Conscious or unconscious, those biases proliferate with each letter combination. Gay men versus lesbians, as just described. Lesbians and gay men versus bisexuals ("Really? Bisexual? Sounds like someone has an identity problem."). Older gays who identify as male or female versus a younger generation that prefers the term "queer" ("Why do you need to create a new term? What does asexual even mean?"). We want to be accepted, and rightfully so, yet we can be anything but fully accepting when it comes to members of our own LGBTQ+ tribe. Our biases against others who aren't like us in the LGBTQ+ community are alive and well. Discrimination, bias, and stereotypes that we can't stand from noncommunity members thrive within the community. It's the part no one says out loud.

It doesn't stop there. Even within a particular letter, when acted on, those biases can be cruel. Karen Blair, writing in *Psychology Today*, observed:

> In a world of dating that often seems to be based upon split-second decisions of swiping one way or another, the communication of dating preferences often seems to get reduced to the simplest and bluntest of terms. On many apps that cater to gay men, it is not uncommon to see headlines that explicitly state the types of people someone is not interested in dating or hooking up with—such as "no fats, no femmes!" Indeed, the devaluation of femininity, or femmephobia, seems to be a common trait of contemporary gay culture.[32]

Bundle all of that up into your briefcase and carry it into the office. Professional decorum might mute it, but it's still there. Last year, the Dallas LGBTQ+ affinity group at EY held a picnic. "What a surprise," said no one, as the lesbians sat on their blankets and the gay men on

---

[32] Karen Blair and Adam Davies, "Is Femmephobia in Gay Culture Contributing to Loneliness?," *Psychology Today*, December 31, 2020, Is Femmephobia in Gay Culture Contributing to Loneliness?

theirs. I don't believe for a second that anyone harbored ill will or bad thoughts about others. We simply gravitated to "our own kind," as my sweet Southern grandmother used to say about another type of minority. We benignly acted on a bias against those who were just enough unlike us to create a discomfort, which led us to gather with the people we saw as more like us. We are not immune from the very thing we are fighting to eradicate in others. Don't you dare turn your bias into prejudice against my people. Only we get to do that.

We All Need to Feel Accepted

Accepting a person's sexuality is about more than simply saying who you sleep with or love is fine. That acceptance—or refusal to accept it—drives decisions about how you interact with that person. It often has real, painful consequences that go beyond a mental mind shift. The only reason the organization The Trevor Project even exists is because there is still a lack of acceptance of LGBTQ youth. Reflect on this from The Trevor Project:

Our Mission: To end suicide among lesbian, gay, bisexual, transgender, queer & questioning young people.

Our Vision: A world where all LGBTQ young people see a bright future for themselves.

Our Goal: To serve 1.8 million crisis contacts annually, by the end of our 25th year, while continuing to innovate on our core services.[33]

---

[33] The Trevor Project, Strategic Plan & Mission | The Trevor Project.

Consider that a mission drives an organization toward its goals. Here the mission is to end suicide among LGBTQ youth by serving a target number of kids in crisis each year. When LGBTQ youth are more than four times more likely to attempt suicide than their peers, the scope of this crisis becomes clearer. And to be equally clear, again from The Trevor Project:

> LGBTQ youth are not inherently prone to suicide risk because of their sexual orientation or gender identity but rather placed at higher risk because of how they are mistreated and stigmatized in society.[34]

What's the connection? The first time we experience acceptance in our lives, even before we're aware of the concept, is from our families. It's the basis for feeling secure and safe within our families. We do whatever we can to protect these needs. According to *Psychology Today*:

> Risk factors specific to sexual minority youth include gender nonconformity, **low (or lack of) family support,** and victimization for being a sexual minority (Mustanski & Liu, 2013). That LGBTQ-IA youth are exposed to these additional risk factors, atop those normally increasing one's risk for suicidal ideation and completed suicide, helps to explain why sexual minority youth are at a greater risk of desiring to end, and sometimes successfully ending, their own lives.[35]

---

[34] The Trevor Project, "Facts About LGBTQ Youth Suicide," December 15, 2021, Facts About LGBTQ Youth Suicide | The Trevor Project.

[35] Katherine Cullen, "Why Are Suicide Rates Higher Among LGBTQ Youth?," *Psychology Today*, October 12, 2017, Why Are Suicide Rates Higher Among LGBTQ Youth? | Psychology Today.

It's the absence—or withdrawal—of that first time we experience acceptance, from our family, that is a major suicide risk factor for LGBTQ+ youth as opposed to their straight counterparts. When we don't experience that acceptance from our families, it affects how we view relationships and how we trust people later in our lives, both personally and professionally.

That trust isn't limited to the individual level either. This is my own theory, and I can only back it up with my own experiences: without that trust established early on to be our true selves, we're sure not going to throw our trust at an organization with something so sensitive, so potentially career-limiting, as our sexuality.

Remember that 46% of LGBTQ+ workers who reported they remain closeted at work? It's not just so they can appear mysterious to coworkers who wonder what they get up to on the weekends. It's because collectively, those coworkers represent the organization, and any one of them at any time could blow their cover—or worse, stop liking them—if they risked revealing their ugly secret. Their bosses could decide they weren't "quite ready" for that promotion without giving them anything more substantive to go on. Clients might assert they're not getting the amount of attention they expect. Whatever the situation, whoever the group, dig beneath the surface of any of those four reasons that Kolmar gave, and you'll hit trust every time.

There's an obvious catch-22 here: how can a gay person trust if they don't feel accepted, but how can they gain acceptance without putting their trust on the line? Even this, on its own, is something straight people don't ever have to think about. Well, I take that back. They may not be accepted for other reasons (maybe they're boring or jerks), but it's not going to be because of who they *love*.

Concentric Circles of Compassion

In 2022, after years of doing their thing with no motive other than to entertain children, events called Drag Queen Story Hour (DQSH) became easy targets for the far right. According to their website, it was created by Michelle Tea in San Francisco in 2015. Its mission "celebrates reading through the glamorous art of drag. Our chapter network creates diverse, accessible, and culturally inclusive family programming where kids can express their authentic selves and become bright lights of change in their communities."[36]

Conservative media outlets slam it as sexualizing children. Right-wing politicians say these outlandishly dressed men continuing a long tradition of dressing up as women are on a mission to groom our children. "Grooming" is an ugly word they know all too well conjures up horrific images of pedophiles slowly and methodically preparing children for sexual assault or worse. No matter that they're using the word incorrectly—they already know that. It's the association between pedophiles and drag queens they want you to make.

In that first job I mentioned earlier, in high-tech, before I came out, a quiet, middle-aged man named Barry (not his real name) worked on my same floor, a few rows down in a different group. He reminds me of that song from *Chicago*, "Mr. Cellophane," whose character sings, "Cause, you can look right through me, Walk, right by me, And never know I'm there." Unremarkable. Indistinguishable. He was just there, doing whatever he did on his little Apple computer, day in and day out, with his wispy gray hair and cardigan sweaters.

---

[36] The Drag Queen Story Hour, About - Drag Queen Story Hour.

One day Barry wasn't there. The story raged up and down the early nineties' corridors: he'd shown up to work in a wig and *ball gown*! He asked to be called by a woman's name instead of his and wanted to change his *badge* to his new image and name. WTF?! Can you believe it? Well, no, actually I can't. Those were the salacious details that had jumped into the story by the time it reached the fourteenth floor. The reality wasn't quite as juicy. Come to find out, Barry was a known local drag queen getting ready to start the gender reassignment process, and he was seen being escorted out by security that morning in front of the earlier arrivals to work. To this day, I don't know how, but somehow the company found out about his upcoming transition, so as soon as he badged in, security was alerted.

Barry was taken into a side room where his manager and HR met with him to explain that he was being let go. I don't know if any reason was given. When we had layoffs, hundreds of people were let go. Not just one. And not one who dressed in women's clothes in his private life for the purpose of singing badly to adoring crowds. By law, the company didn't need to give a reason—like most of us in America, Barry was an at-will employee. At-will employment is an employer-employee agreement in which a worker can be fired or dismissed for any reason, without warning or explanation. To be fair, it also means that an employee can leave their job without giving a reason or warning.

At-will employment agreements come with a few caveats, the most important to the employee involves wrongful termination. This can happen for a few reasons, the most common one focuses on whether the employer discriminated against the employee when letting them go.

Dry stuff in principle. At that time, LGBTQ+ protections didn't exist. It might still be discriminatory, but employment law didn't see it that way. I could have been fired for being gay. Barry was certainly fired for being a transgender soon-to-be-transexual. Lesbians and gays were, relatively speaking, more accepted than transgendered and transexuals. Back then, even without those legal protections, and when simply being gay was still illegal in Texas, I think there would have been much more of an uproar if I or any other gay man or lesbian had been fired from their white-collar job because of their sexual orientation. While televangelists were still preaching about our eternal damnation to hell, the abomination of homosexuality, etc., we were becoming less of a nebulous "other" and more a brother, aunt, friend, and yeah, coworker. We had people who stood up for us and supported us, even if they weren't always sure how. Who was there for Barry in his cardigan sweater? As far as I know, he never filed a wrongful-dismissal lawsuit. It didn't make the local Dallas news. I don't know if he successfully transitioned. I didn't stand up for him, and I didn't bother to find out anything else about the situation. You know, just in case it made *me* look suspicious.

Where was my compassion for him? Just like with that kid in seventh grade back in Chapter 1, I was looking out for yours truly. My desire to survive an imagined scenario where I was lumped in with him smothered any compassion I might have had for him and his situation. Even though this was before the internet and there wasn't likely much I could do to find out more about him, I didn't want to even try. This was back in the day when we were all just the gays and lesbians. It was pre-letter times. Before we became the LGB community, then the LGBT one, and so on. Those letters mean we're all in it together. That we have each other's backs. At that time, I couldn't imagine that Barry and I had anything at all in common. I could feel for what my fellow gay men were going through in their struggles to come out, how they were treated at work, and what their families thought of them. While I couldn't imagine being attracted to a woman, I could still overlay my feelings on a lesbian's general experience. I didn't get bisexuality at all, but still, we were on the man/woman spectrum of attraction. The transgendered folks occupied a world of their own that I didn't even attempt to understand.

And while a lot has changed in these thirty years since that experience, for many of us, this relativistic compassion, these concentric circles of compassion, remain. Straight people generally feel more compassionate toward gays and lesbians, less toward bisexuals, and even less toward the transgendered. Straight people know more gays and lesbians, fewer bisexuals, and fewer still transgendered people.

Just like that earlier *Modern Family* example, it's not just the lack of understanding and compassion between the straight and LGBTQ+ worlds. Even within our own, there are biases, stereotypes, and judgments. And I'm not talking about gays versus lesbians. Extending that compassion outside our own circle is often a tall order. Gay men will refer to themselves as "masculine" or "straight-acting," the implication being that the opposite of those traits is a less desirable state of being, less attractive to another gay man battling his own sense of self-worth based on how he compares in outward behavior to a straight man. "Baby butch," "lipstick lesbian," and "stone butch" circulate among the lesbian vernacular, and so on.

The LGBTQ+ community isn't unique among tribes. Every tribe has its language, customs, and unwritten rules. It's ironic, however, that we expect and even demand compassion from others while exhibiting stingy behavior with it inside our own tribe. If we expect it from others—and we have every right to—it might help if we practice it more with each other first.

Reflection

If you are not straight . . .

- What words do you use to describe people in the LGBTQ+ community who are different from you?

- What words do you use to describe yourself?

- What assumptions have you made about other LGBTQ+ people?

- What assumptions do you think others make about you?

- Do you feel accepted just as you are? How do you know?

If you are straight . . .

- In general, what are the differences between you and someone who identifies as LGBTQ+? What are the similarities?

- What assumptions do you think LGBTQ+ people make about you?

- Have you done or said something to an LGBTQ+ person that you wish you hadn't done or said? What happened and what did you do about it?

- Do you accept others just as they are? How do you know?

10

Cultural Distinctions and Transformations

A discussion about transforming gay bias to gay advancement in corporate America must recognize that most corporations today hold multiple passports. While this book addresses biases and challenges of working as an LGBTQ+ person in corporate America, as these corporations expand evermore globally, they develop more global stances on a wide range of issues that matter to them and their stakeholders: environment, family, food, gender and racial equality, governance, health, terrorism. And human rights. According to the United Nations:

> Human rights are rights inherent to all human beings, regardless of race, sex, nationality, ethnicity, language, religion, or any other status. Human rights include the right to life and liberty, freedom from slavery and torture, freedom of opinion and expression, the right to work and education, and many more. Everyone is entitled to these rights, without discrimination.[37]

---

[37] United Nations, "Global Issues: Human Rights," Human Rights | United Nations.

When I started writing this book, my thoughts coalesced around the injustices and biases that we in the LGBTQ+ community face working in the US. While this has been the focus, I knew I wanted to write a chapter that, at a high level, compared our struggles in this country to those of our fellow LGBTQ+ peers in other parts of the world. I knew we had it relatively *good*, but I wasn't prepared for how *bad* it was elsewhere.

As a gay man, I described working at EY as living in a bubble. Whatever prejudices or microaggressions I might have experienced in the "real" world vanished as soon as I badged in (or logged on during the pandemic and beyond). It was a beautiful world that was aggressively intolerant of anti-LGBTQ+ behavior. There were issues, to be sure. Each location had its own subculture that local culture influenced: it was easier to be out in the New York City office than in the Birmingham, Alabama, one. But regardless of where you worked, overall, the firm actively and consistently supported a safe environment where choosing to be out was a nonissue, irrespective of whatever personal issues you might be facing. While I have no hard data, I hope this environment means the 46% of people who are closeted at work (as cited in Chapter 8) is much lower in the EYs of the world. I should probably more precisely say the EYs of the *Western world*.

The Impact of Empire

Before jumping into the unsettling truth of what it's like to be LGBTQ+ in other parts of the world, it's useful to understand the origins of draconian anti-LGBTQ+ laws and penalties in those places. Let's use the United Kingdom as an example. While other European powers colonized lands across the globe, it was the nature of British law that uniquely positioned it to pass on to its empire the discriminatory laws that, ironically, no longer exist in Britain itself.

According to the London-based Human Dignity Trust:

> British law is by some way the largest source of criminalization. The country was prolific in spreading provisions criminalizing same-sex sexual activity to its colonies. More than half of countries which criminalize LGBT people today can trace the source of their law to Britain, either as a former colony or "protectorate," or another historical relationship. Provisions include "buggery," "unnatural offences," and "indecency," while "cross-dressing" and other laws criminalizing gender expression also largely find their origins in British colonial law.
>
> Not only did Britain export laws criminalizing LGBT people, but the broader sexual offence regime imposed on colonized states was, and continues to be, discriminatory against other marginalized groups including women, children, and people with disabilities.
>
> Other colonial powers such as France and Spain, whose legal systems were heavily influenced by the Napoleonic code which did not criminalize same-sex sexual activity, did not have such a lasting impact in terms of anti-LGBT laws.[38]

---

[38] Human Dignity Trust, "A History of LGBT Criminalisation, Over 500 years of Outlawing Lesbian, Gay, Bisexual and Transgender People," Human Dignity Trust, A History of LGBT Criminalisation | Human Dignity Trust.

What's It Like to Be Gay In . . .

An article on the Human Rights Watch website perfectly captures the reasons that the LGBTQ community faces startling levels of bias and bigotry around the world:

> When authorities use religion, culture, or tradition to curtail gender expression or sexual orientation, they usually invoke a collective and singular authority: a narrowly defined concept of the family, a static culture, or a singular religious orthodoxy. And yet the real issue is not culture, but bodily autonomy, the right to make choices about one's own body. This is a major reason why LGBT rights have become a battleground between pluralism, which liberal democracy promotes, and populist authoritarian rule, which pits individual rights against majoritarian group norms.[39]

According to the Pew Research Center, in North America and Western Europe, the percentage of people who say homosexuality should be accepted by society ranges from a low of 72% in the US (surprise!) to 94% in Sweden. Contrast that with 7% in Nigeria, where homosexuality is punishable by up to 14 years in prison, and 14% in Russia.[40] There, in late 2022, Vladimir Putin signed into law

---

[39] Graeme Reid, "A Year of Challenges and Some Successes for LGBT People," Human Rights Watch, June 14, 2022,
A Year of Challenges and Some Successes for LGBT People | Human Rights Watch (hrw.org).

[40] Jacob Poushter and Nicholas Kent, "The Global Divide on Homosexuality Persists," Pew Research Center, June 25, 2020, Views of Homosexuality Around the World | Pew Research Center.

a bill banning Russians from promoting or "praising" homosexual relationships or publicly suggesting that they are "normal." It also prohibits "propaganda" of pedophilia and gender reassignment in advertising, books, films. The original version of the law adopted in 2013 banned "propaganda of nontraditional sexual relations" among minors. Now it applies to adults too.[41]

Imagine getting busted in Russia for saying two women who love each other have a wonderful relationship. Well, now you can. Nothing fills a gulag up faster than absurd laws that are grossly open to interpretation.

And consider this from the 2022 World Population Review:

> Only 5% of the United Nations member states have written into their constitutions that sexual orientation-based discrimination is prohibited. These states include Ecuador, Mexico, Portugal, Bolivia, South Africa, Sweden, and Nepal. Most of Europe and South America have taken steps to tackle sexual orientation-based discrimination in the workplace, as well as some other countries around the world. In general, same-sex couples are not allowed to adopt outside the Americas, Europe, and Australia and New Zealand.
>
> The Netherlands was the first country to allow same-sex marriage in 2001 and Ecuador is the most recent

---

[41] Uliana Pavlova, "Russia's State Duma Passes Law Banning 'LGBT Propaganda'," CNN, November 24, 2022, Russia's State Duma passes law banning 'LGBT propaganda'.

country to legalize it. Same-sex marriage is not legalized in the majority of Eastern Europe, Africa, and Asia. Only 13% of UN member states have legalized gay marriage and a handful recognize civil unions, including Peru, Greece, and Italy.[42]

And this advice to travelers, from the UK Government's Foreign and Commonwealth Office's website:

- If you receive unwelcome attention or unwelcome remarks about your sexuality or gender identity, it's usually best to ignore them and move to a safe place. Depending on the country or area you're in, you may then want to report it to the authorities.

- In some countries, you may be more likely to experience difficulties in rural areas so it's best to exercise more discretion.

- Some hotels, especially in rural areas, may refuse bookings from same-sex couples—check before you go.[43]

If you're a straight person, imagine having to beef up your pretravel list based on that guidance. Passport—check. Phone charger—check. Two hotel rooms in Kissmyass, Nowhere—check.

---

[42] 2022 World Population Review.

[43] Foreign & Commonwealth Office and Foreign, Commonwealth & Development Office, "Lesbian, Gay, Bisexual, and Transgender Foreign Travel Advice," Gov. UK, March 22, 2013, last updated June 27, 2022,
Lesbian, Gay, Bisexual and Transgender foreign travel advice - GOV.UK (www.gov.uk).

Not that most of us want to travel to a place where we'd be greeted with such a chilly welcome. That's not the point. It's that we must think about it at all.

So, what does any of this data have to do with where you work? Well, everything. I loved my corporate bubble, but it was just that. It was an environment filled with rarefied air—cleaner, purer, nicer to breathe than outside. And it was a bubble inside a country with a relatively advanced view of homosexuality *overall*. The US government isn't going to cart us away in the middle of the night for sleeping in the same bed. The American Airlines Center in Dallas hosts basketball, hockey, and concerts but not open-to-the-general-population stoning events for gays.

The general culture of a country directly influences the culture of the company where one works, whether it's an international or local one. And because it's pretty easy to be gay in the US, despite rumblings from fringe populists and politicians, it's easier to be gay at work, comparatively speaking. Likewise, being gay and out in the Saudi Arabia office of EY is a far different and, I suspect, far rarer occurrence. This despite the fact that most large global organizations have global DEI policies.

What if you're an organization that operates in one of these countries? Or conducts business with organizations that do? It's easy to put that rainbow flag background on your LinkedIn profile if you live in a gay-friendly country. It's not so easy if you're in most of Africa, where antidiscrimination laws concerning sexual orientation are mostly nonexistent. Which is a big rainbow-colored red herring anyway, since in these same countries, it's illegal to be gay. As noted earlier, Nigeria serves up a healthy prison term for being gay. But double-click on that data, and you find that in several states within Nigeria, it's punishable by death. And capital punishment for being gay is hardly rare. According to Generation for Rights Over the World (GROW):

> Capital punishment still concerns 12 countries in the world, all located on the African and Asian continents: Afghanistan, Saudi Arabia, Brunei, United Arab Emirates, Iran, Mauritania, Nigeria (in the 12 northern states that have adopted Sharia law), Pakistan, Qatar (applies only to Muslims), Somalia (in states which have adopted Sharia law, i.e., the Islamic emirates of Al-Shabaab), Sudan and Yemen.
>
> In Sudan, men are sentenced to death the first time around, while the death penalty does not apply to women until the fourth repeat of the crime (the sentence is 100 lashes for the first three times).[44]

Only 100 lashes? Okay. But even in countries where it's not officially a capital crime to be gay, vigilante executions, beatings, and torture are unofficially tolerated.

What about those places where it's on the books but not officially enforced? Isn't that progress, relatively speaking? Using information again from The Human Dignity Trust, I'm not so sure:

> Criminalization has a number of damaging effects on

---

[44] Camille Cottais, "Gay rights around the World: Where Are We At?" Generation for Rights Over the World (GROW), January 28, 2021, Gay rights around the world: where are we at? - Grow Think Tank.

LGBT people. Most obviously, criminalization means that LGBT people can be lawfully arrested, detained, and prosecuted simply for being who they are. When in detention LGBT people are vulnerable to further abuses, including verbal harassment, physical assault, sexual violence, and the denial of healthcare and legal representation. Countless examples of torture and other types of ill-treatment of detained LGBT people in criminalizing countries have been documented.

Even where laws are not enforced, the mere existence of these provisions has deeply harmful effects on LGBT people. Criminalizing provisions are used both by law enforcement and the public to harass, threaten, and extort LGBT people. Their existence perpetuates stigma and prejudice, providing tacit approval of discrimination and violence against LGBT people. Under these legal regimes LGBT people are excluded from society, and feel unable to report crimes for fear of abuse and arrest by police officers. Furthermore, there is no guarantee that the laws won't be enforced in future.[45]

Pretty grim stuff. You're sure not going to be out at work if doing so could get you arrested, beaten up, raped, or worse. But progress *is* being made all around the world. Introduced in 2021, Angola's new penal code included antidiscrimination protections for LGBTQ

---

[45] Human Dignity Trust, "LGBT People & the Law," Human Dignity Trust, LGBT people & the law | Human Dignity Trust.

people. Bhutan decriminalized same-sex conduct. In South Korea, a court ruled that the country's military ban on same-sex conduct is discriminatory and unconstitutional. Chile's parliament voted in favor of same-sex marriage, as did the citizens of Cuba.

LGTBQ progress around the world—two steps forward, 1.9 steps back. So, what is the moral and ethical role of global organizations that conduct business in countries that are not LGBTQ+-friendly? They can't encourage their employees to bring their full selves to work if doing so gets them imprisoned or killed. Creating an open and accepting workplace environment takes a lot of time, energy, and persistence that may not be worth it if it's so far removed from the realities of the local culture that no one's going to be out in that workplace anyway.

No single answer is going to apply to every culture, religion, or historical context. And this book focuses on the many challenges that LGBTQ+ folks face in corporate America. I don't have the mental or emotional strength to delve into that answer at a global level. Even so, at a bare minimum, everyone should be free from worry about physical or emotional harm in their workplace because of their sexuality. In or out of the closet, individuals who work in global organizations should be treated with the same fundamental respect for life and dignity, whether they are based in Canada or Cameroon. I know they aren't. And yet, that's not really a very high bar, is it?

Reflection

If you are not straight . . .

- What decisions about travel might you make that are influenced by your sexual orientation?

- Have you ever traveled for work to a country where it was illegal to be LGBTQ+? What did it feel like?

- Have you ever told your employer that you won't travel to a particular country because of its treatment of LGBTQ+ people?

- Have you ever had a negative experience when traveling outside the US that was due to your sexual orientation? What happened?

- To what extent is it acceptable for shared religious beliefs to influence a nation's laws or policies?

If you are straight . . .

- Does a country's laws or customs related to the LGBTQ+ community affect your travel decisions? If so, how? If not, why not?

- Have you ever traveled for work to a country where it was illegal to be LGBTQ+? How did you know it was illegal?

- When traveling outside the US, have you ever seen someone mistreated because of their sexuality? What happened?

- To what extent is it acceptable for shared religious beliefs to influence a nation's laws or policies?

11

The Global Awakening

I don't see it as much in movie trailers today, but there was a time when the phrase "In a world . . . " seemed to be the intro monologue for every movie trailer. It was an easy way to set the scene of an alternate reality, a past that we needed to be reminded of, or a dystopian future. When I see mass shootings in gay clubs, drag queens being accused of grooming children, and parents who support their transgender children being accused of child abuse, I think about "In a world."

In a world where you can marry who you love. In a world where you're not thrown in jail for being gay. In a world where every person is free of fear of being 100 percent who they are.

There are infinite worlds like this rolling around in my head. A world where you aren't executed, tortured, or imprisoned because of your sexuality. A world where you don't make travel plans based on where you and your same-sex spouse might be arrested for sleeping in the same bed. A world where it's not just okay to be gay, a world where it doesn't matter at all.

Super realistic. It's unfortunate that one's sexuality is always going to matter to various groups of people, but here we are. And I haven't written this book to change the world. So, what might we dare to dream about that *can* become a reality in our lifetimes? *What if we lived in a world where . . .*

What if. "What if they find out" kicked off this book? Such a frightening thought for a twelve-year-old kid who knew no one would love him if they found out. Knew that he'd be teased even more, *if.* That God would never forgive such a horrific sin, *if. What if* took me to the worst-case scenarios about my sexuality.

What if. In my coaching practice, I've come to appreciate even more the positive, healing power of a what-if question. The same words that keep frightened kids—and adults—from embracing their true selves even today can also inspire the imagination to explore the best-case scenarios. *What if you could start over again? What if that obstacle was not in your way? What if you had that difficult conversation?*

What if. One of my favorite quotes comes from C.S. Lewis, who said, "You can't go back and change the beginning, but you can start where you are and change the ending." While we can't actually start over at the beginning, we can reboot starting from where we are today. The force that drives the desire to change the ending comes from those two words. *What if.*

As I researched and wrote this book, I found myself asking what-if questions in response to the information that made its way to these pages, and I wrote them down. Here is my what-if list that powers my dreams of what can become a reality in our lifetime, what can change the ending.

- What if gay kids grew up certain that they were unconditionally loved?

- What if all kids grew up respecting others just as they are?

- What if we didn't worry about people finding out about us?

- What if we challenged negative notions about being gay?

- What if we embraced more opportunities to educate?

- What if we didn't have to come out more than once?

- What if coming out weren't a thing?

- What if we didn't have to filter out our sexuality?

- What if senior leadership were more like us?

- What if compassion weren't a limited commodity?

What if gay kids grew up certain that they were unconditionally loved?

If you knew I was gay, you wouldn't love/like me. Yes, this still happens. Kids still get kicked out of their homes for being gay. Conversion therapy still happens. Gay kids still have a higher suicide rate than straight kids. Preachers still preach that being gay, as an abomination, is worse than any other sin by far in the Scriptures. Yet these are symptoms of the underlying problem: we grow up believing the worst thing in the world that could happen to us is that our parents find out we're gay.

Security and confidence in the existence of unconditional love, on the other hand, negate the fear of not being loved. When we know others love us, we love ourselves. We love who we are. We grow up making decisions that don't factor our sexuality into the equation. Our focus shifts from fear to confidence. We're more confident in our whole lives, personally and professionally. We make career and employment decisions based on our passions for what we love to do, not where we might be accepted or tolerated. We advance professionally like everyone else advances in imperfect organizations. We aren't afraid that being gay is a barrier to being successful.

What if all kids grew up respecting others just as they are?

During my senior year in high school, the homecoming queen got more votes by far than any other nominee for a simple reason: she was nice—always nice—to everyone. Whatever *Breakfast Club* clique you belonged to was irrelevant to her. I don't think it ever occurred to her not to be nice to everyone. And I remember this because no one else was like this in school, myself included. We all were unkind in some way, large or small, to others who weren't like us. It made me feel better about my perceived shortcomings. I looked better when I put others down. I didn't respect myself because I was a closeted gay. How could I respect others? But that was me. Kids become aware of differences early on and pounce on them in others. I suspect it's primarily because of their own insecurities, fueled by beliefs that they learn as they grow.

Respect for ourselves that is instilled in us as children drives deeper respect for others. If we take that a step further and say that respecting others means, among other things, that we accept them for who they are, then who cares in seventh grade if you're gay? And if you don't have those childhood experiences of being bullied because you're gay, or even perceived to be gay, you aren't bringing that baggage to adulthood. If you are straight and spent your childhood years respecting others, your behavior will be less likely to lead you down a path of unkindness. Gay and straight people enter an adult world where they don't see each other through that junior-high lens. We work side by side. One doesn't worry about what the other thinks. The other simply sees another human being.

What would it be like to carry that same view from this alternate-universe childhood into adulthood? What if you showed up at work every day being entirely who you are, bringing your 100 percent authentic self, because who you had a crush on, who you loved as a younger version of yourself, didn't matter?

What if we didn't worry about people finding out about us?

This one's the other side of the self-respect coin. If we had it, we wouldn't care. We wouldn't convince ourselves that our world would come crashing down around us if "they" knew. A world we carefully created to keep others from finding out about us in the first place, curated from the ruins of memories of others who didn't follow the rules. Those intricate frameworks of facades and illusions representing the life we squeezed and squished ourselves into rather than the life we desired, the life that fits. Sure, it's illogical, but who has time for logic when primal fear drives every aspect of our behavior?

No worries about being found out, or worse, outed. No decision diamonds. No deciding which conversation path to take based on who knows what about us. Our lives don't run on multiple operating systems. There's only one platform, one system, one database. I bring my authentic self to a meeting, a party, to church, to the office. It's all the same me. I've got energy at the end of the day because I'm not running multiple versions of myself. I'm authentic, and from this authenticity emerges emotions, thoughts, and feelings that are in harmony with my singular life.

What if we challenged negative notions about being gay?

How many times have we heard words like "faggot," "queer," "sissy," "tranny," and "dyke" said in front of us and we've said nothing? What if someone asked me who the man is in our relationship, and I had the presence of mind to ask them to be more explicit about what they mean by that question? Or my personal favorite, how can I be a Christian and gay?

This is tough, especially if we're in a situation where we fear for our safety. That's not the time to tell some thug that we don't appreciate being called a faggot, nor do I recommend you do it then either. There have been safer times, however, when I've heard words or seen gestures in reference to others and have said nothing. It was assumed that I was straight, which created a safe environment for bigotry, and my deafening silence created a perceived safe environment for me as well. Sometimes I've challenged them. More often than not, I'm ashamed to say, I haven't. The fight's not in me on that day, or I don't feel like wasting my energy where it won't change anything, or if I'm brutally honest with myself, I don't want to create an awkward situation. Even though it's awkward for me, I give the other person a pass to *spare them*. What the hell, Kev?

What if on just one of those occasions, I decided their awkwardness was not my problem? What if that same awkwardness created some tiny breakthrough in understanding? What if it *might* have changed something? What if we each did it on that one day when we didn't really feel like it?

What if we embraced more opportunities to educate?

This one builds on, but is distinct from, challenging negative notions. Finding oneself being called a homo in a dark alley is probably not the best moment to try to educate our stalker. I believe, however, that more people just don't understand what it's like to be LGBTQ+. Their comments may be clunky, but I don't think they're intentionally malicious. And maybe it shouldn't be our lot in life, but if I don't take this opportunity to help them learn, then whose responsibility is it?

On the flip side of the dark alley, if I thought someone was genuinely curious, albeit misguided, about who the man was in our relationship, I might pause to understand their intention and explain that gay relationships aren't based on a heterosexual template of body parts. No one plays the man or the woman in a non-straight relationship. That's a mind-blowing concept for many straight people because it's been their only point of reference in their own relationships. Again, benign, if not a bit misguided. What opportunity do I have to help them understand me better? What opportunity will I have passed up if I choose not to help them understand? Give a man a fish, and he can eat for a day. Teach a man to fish . . .

189

What if we didn't have to come out more than once?

We've already talked about what it's like to come out to different people at different points in your life and your career—your employer, your friends, your clients, suppliers, and so on. It's exhausting. Watching for the signs, wondering what the reaction might be, considering its impact on the business relationship. Then there are the mind games. "Come on, Kev. You're blowing this way out of proportion," even though a lifetime of encounters like this has taught me to proceed with extreme caution.

I suppose one option is to include something in introductions like, "Hi, I'm Kevin. On behalf of my big ole gay husband and me, it's nice to meet you." It addresses the elephant in the room, albeit a tad socially awkward, so I dream more of a time when people don't see my wedding ring and assume I'm married to a woman. Or make no assumptions at all and show genuine interest in my life outside of work. Wait, it's more than that, although it's that as well. It's that we wouldn't have to worry about coming out more than once, as we discussed in Chapter 6, because we wouldn't come out at all. It wouldn't be called anything. You'd just tell your client, coworker, boss, supplier, or whoever, that you had a husband, wife, or no significant other in your life, and it wouldn't matter what sex either of you were. No one would care, so you wouldn't care either.

What if coming out weren't a thing?

The endgame is that mentioning you have a husband, or wife, or that you're transgendered, or whatever, is such a dull piece of information that the term "coming out" has lost all its meaning. Now wouldn't that be something? "Mom, Dad, I'm afraid I have something to tell you," transforms to, "Mom, Dad, I know I mentioned I'm going out with that cute girl I met last summer at cheerleader camp. You never listen to me!"

Just imagine the variations on the classic birds and bees talk. My favorite client might not, after learning I'm gay, ask me to be her gay best friend. Your dad's best friend would run into him at Home Depot and comment on what a looker his daughter's same-sex girlfriend is. It's still a sexist comment, but not a homophobic one. Choose your battles.

What if we didn't have to filter out our sexuality?

Back to that decision diamond and who knows what about us already. Having a great time back in my twenties, floating down the Guadalupe River on weekends with all my newish gay friends, inner tubes, and beer, and then showing up at work on Monday with a sunburn. "Wow, you got some sun this weekend. What did you do?"

"Oh, this? Just hung out with some friends at the apartment pool."

While it's painfully tempting to tell a straight coworker who repeatedly talks about his wife that I don't need him to get all political about his sex life, it would be more fun if every one of us in the LGBTQ+ community could talk about our love lives, or lack of one, just like straight people do. What's stopping us? You don't want me shoving my sexuality down your throat, remember? I never said that. Wait, what?!

A bit of humor as I pull back from my little diatribe there. Anyway, aside from the multiple microdecisions we make about who to tell what, it's exhausting. The bars in that battery indicator drop fast when we expend enormous amounts of energy making split-second decisions about how much to filter out of our stories.

If we didn't have to filter out our sexuality, we wouldn't need to recharge our batteries quite so often. Our friends and colleagues would know what we did on the weekends, and we wouldn't care even if they did. So what? It's never been directly about whether we cared. We only care because we're afraid others do, which underpins the need for so many filters in the first place. Maybe the real what-if here is: *What if we didn't give a shit what others thought about us?*

What if senior leadership were more like us?

What if fewer people in the LGBTQ+ community didn't self-select out of the corporate ladder? What difference does it make if I see a lesbian, a transgendered man, or a self-identified bisexual in the C-suite? The answer to either of those questions feels theoretical, since we make up a tiny fraction of people in VP and C-suite positions. People in the LGBTQ+ community frequently question the sincerity of their employers' commitment to them because people like them rarely make it as far as the boardroom.

If you're a straight white person reading this, and you were looking for a new job, how would you react to learning that the board of your prospective employer was composed entirely of Black people? What might that tell you about your opportunities for advancement at that

192

organization? No one looks like you at the most senior levels, but hey, maybe you'll be the first. It shouldn't really matter anyway, right?

If senior leadership included more people like us, it would set off a chain reaction. More people like us would want to work for those organizations, so more of us would apply and be hired. Once inside, we'd likely stay longer because we'd know we have a real chance of making it to the top, if that's what we want. By staying longer, more of us would reach middle- and upper-level management and, finally, senior leadership. There would be more of us at all levels of the organization, driving a virtuous cycle of inspiration for the next generation.

What if compassion weren't a limited commodity?

It's easy to feel compassion for people and situations that we already relate to. It's familiar. We've been there; we've walked in their shoes. We understand what they're going through. It's harder to feel it when we can't relate. Extending compassion to someone you don't approve of, like, or understand can be difficult.

There's a certain "theyness" mentality to how we allocate compassion. The more a person is like us, the more compassion we allocate. The more that person is a they and not like us, the stricter we become with how we dole it out. In our world, the idea of compassion as an unlimited quantity is mind-blowing, but it doesn't have to be. It's in each of us, and it is limitless.

What are your what-ifs?